Selected Poems

Dennis Finnell

FUTURECYCLE PRESS

www.futurecycle.org

Cover x-ray image by Mikael Häggström, used with permission; author photo by Anita Finnell; cover and interior book design by Diane Kistner; Gentium Book Basic with Cronos Pro titling

Library of Congress Control Number: 2020945353

Published by FutureCycle Press
Athens, GA

ISBN 978-1-952593-00-0

For Anita

Contents

from
THE GAUGUIN ANSWER SHEET

from
PIE 8

from
RUINS ASSEMBLING

Foreword

This welcome collection gathers a substantial and judicious sampling of work from Dennis Finnell's five books. Like Wallace Stevens he was well into middle age when his first book appeared (*Red Cottage*, 1991)—so his poetic character was already largely formed. The present volume represents something like four decades' worth of inventive, surprising, and moving poetry. Re-reading these five collections, which differ from each other in a number of ways, I was nonetheless struck most by how well they all bear the unmistakable signature of their own author, who, also like Stevens, often blends philosophical speculation with linguistic hijinks.

To borrow an assertion from Stevens, "all poetry is experimental poetry." Dennis Finnell has taken that maxim to heart, demonstrating an ever-restless spirit over a goodly variety of forms and subjects. He favors free verse, though he can write a fine sestina or ballade when he wants to. His books assume a number of distinct incarnations. The earliest lyrics in *Red Cottage* represent, as is common with first books, many years of work as the poet discovered his voice and reckoned with his origins and obsessions. "Taking Leave of St. Louis" introduced one lifelong theme, his continual returning, in memory as well as real time, to the city of his birth, a place he has never taken leave of. Stylistically, he ranges in *Red Cottage* from an earthy, mythic tone that can remind you of Charles Simic—

> Because she believes in God
> I will sneeze three times on Tuesday.
> Because he picks his teeth with a matchstick
> I will believe in God.

to a more flowing, expansive mode that perhaps shows some influence of Stevens, as in the stanza concluding the book's opening poem, "The Cloud of Unknowing"—

> Lake Michigan flashes sunlight from its face,
> and a long ore boat pulls the widening
> V of its wake, floating on nothing
> but water, and all of the words for water.

All in all it was a mature and auspicious debut, winning the Juniper Prize at the University of Massachusetts.

Two ambitious book-length suites, *Belovèd Beast* (1995) and *The Gauguin Answer Sheet* (2001), followed *Red Cottage,* each expanding Finnell's range considerably. The author described *Belovèd Beast* as "An American travelogue of sorts," featuring a loosely Whitmanic journey across an

America both mythic and all-too-real, including "encounters along the way with... Rip Van Winkle, Humphrey Bogart's Nick in *Knock on Any Door*, an ersatz Huck Finn working the tourists in Hannibal," and more. Finnell summarized the book's themes as follows: "these poems are about being an ego, an *I*, America's most highly mythologized product, and how being this American self increasingly means being isolated, a party of one. I suppose the belovèd beast is me, is us, our country, our selves, and the poems...trace out the figures of the beast—lyrical, social, cultural." As that description suggests, one of Finnell's trademarks is the permeable membrane he maintains between fictive and real, dream and waking life, past and present, figures from literature and from his own genealogy. Naturally we find him returning to his home place in this book as well. In fact, his cross-country journey commences with "Headless Horseman," whose opening line is, "I come from St. Louis."

The Gauguin Answer Sheet constitutes a further expansion of concerns, broadening from matters of national and personal character to universals of the human condition. More about this unusual book shortly.

After *Gauguin* came the lean, fragmented "erasure" lyrics of Pie 8 (2012). At first blush it would seem that *Pie 8,* Finnell's most radical foray into experimentation, might comprise an outlier, a one-off, and in certain ways that seems true. It is a book of salvaged fragments, images and ideas accumulated over many years, then assembled and partially erased, resulting in a disjointed, non-linear sort of lyric very different from the conversational cadences and long flowing lines of his other books.

Some lines from "To return" will give the book's flavor. It happens to be yet another returning-to-St.-Louis poem, in this case visiting an aged father, who is deaf in one ear. The poem begins—

> To wake to cicadas again
> insect palmists
>
> To open a door
>   August
> all over you
>   having missed you

—and ends:

> to suck on a screened porch
> hidden in sweat   your animal
>
> To whisper sweet on the deaf side

Such lines may seem baffling—would you have guessed St. Louis? deaf father? had I not told you?—yet when you recite this book's pieces aloud the recognizable Finnell music rises through the erasures, along with many of the same themes and obsessions, however obliquely presented.

Finally we find the lively, ever-inventive lyrics of his most recent and probably strongest collection, *Ruins Assembling* (2014), which manages to incorporate all of his stylistic signatures into a tightly crafted, complex collection spanning a variety of themes. All the poems, different as they are from each other and from those in previous books, sound just like Finnell.

By which I mean, book to book his poetic voice features among other virtues a potent gift for both metaphor and description, a winning rough-hewn music, a Whitman-like exploration of the full register of English diction, from earthy to cerebral, oddball humor popping up at serious moments, and surprises aplenty. A 2018 interview points to what makes his poetry both distinctive and distinctively resistant to summary. Asked what writers have influenced him he replied, "Two writers I do read over and over are Chekhov and Dickinson," adding that "they may not influence the way I write now, but how I am composed in the world." Dickinson clearly is no model in terms of poetic form, but is in certain habits of mind—particularly a fondness for tackling large abstractions (selfhood, memory, heritage, and so on) and in telling his truths slantwise, with sharp observation and a healthy respect for the unknown.

Chekhov seems relevant in a couple respects to how Finnell is "composed in the world." Structurally, one feature is the way Finnell, like the great Russian, avoids spurious or even traditional closure. He also thrives more on questions than answers, another notably Chekhovian habit. Thus the contemporary American anecdotal epiphany poem, delivering its moment of transcendence or wisdom at the end, is relatively rare in Finnell's oeuvre. His poems tend to wander and circle back, and are seldom "plotted" conventionally though they are full of narrative elements. As such they can be very resistant to summary and hard to fairly excerpt. Their effects play out on a large canvas. And much of the work in completing each poem, as with Chekhov's tales, is left to the reader. Finnell orchestrates imagery, speculation, description and action— and we readers participate in the performance, entertaining the speaker's "what-ifs" and "maybes" and coming to our own conclusions, as we will.

We see this sort of structural feature most vividly in his book-length poem *The Gauguin Answer Sheet,* which "takes as pretext," Finnell informs us, Paul Gauguin's massive allegorical canvas titled "Where Do We Come From? What Are We? Where Are We Going?" The book poses each of these primal philosophical questions repeatedly, in different contexts, with various provisional answers supplied, contradicted, modified, and repeated. He talks back to the figures in the painting (including a dog), listens to what they have to say, and ranges far and wide in matters of identity, aesthetics, history, and culture. The history includes his own family history, both autobiographical and imagined. The resultant whole is symphonic rather than narrative.

Early to late, it's tempting to call many of his poems meditative, for the way they often take a premise or initiating image and let implications and possibilities spool out unpredictably, peering at the subject from various angles, looping back to the starting point and setting forth in a new direction. To be sure his can be an unhurried, often ruminative style, but those terms may suggest something more low-key than is the case, as well as too solemn. But while he routinely tackles large questions, what a word like "meditative" doesn't capture is how funny his poems can be, at times how zany. True, thinkers like Diogenes and Epictetus make cameo appearances, and allusions to Ovid, Shakespeare, Coleridge, Wordsworth, Mandlestam, Berryman, and other literary icons thread through the book, but Finnell is just as likely to set a meditation on the national character ("The Generic Manifesto") in a Burger King, conducting a cheeky and delicious meditation over his Whopper. Or he will recount a family anecdote (real, imagined—who cares?) in which the speaker's parents separately cook up different sexual pranks to play on each other, with a hilarious payoff that neither they nor the reader sees coming.

Finnell's great fondness for the what-ifs of an examined life puts me in mind also of a poet probably few would compare him to, Robert Frost. Like Frost, Finnell is not often a poet of unalloyed celebration and joy. His is a highly skeptical intelligence with an ultimately dark view of life. Yet there is joy, and humor, lurking under any sadness, leavening it, and expressed most often in his relish for language and its many shenanigans. Frost in an essay describes "woes flat and final," but then concludes, "And then to play. The play's the thing. All virtue in 'as if.'"

That is why, though Finnell trades frequently in woes flat and final, I never find his work depressing, because it is simultaneously so light on its feet, so in love with life's manifold as-ifs. Many of his poems are too long to excerpt effectively, but perhaps a brief glance at a relatively straightforward poem from *Ruins Assembling* may help illustrate his characteristic moves. "The Fitzsimmons Fund" is a letter addressed to "Uncle Vern," who, it turns out, has died and named the poet as one of many beneficiaries; he is entitled to an oddly specific inheritance of $714.23. The poem is at once a meditation on the notion of legacy and identity, and a portrait of his Uncle Vern, a high-rolling gambler who

...in rolled-up shirtsleeves
could eat a rib eye *this thick* everyday at The Turf Club,
keeping an eye on your winners
down below crossing the time between uncertainty and fact,
not always winning, but never losing.
After each race three fingers of the best whiskey all around, on you.

Later it becomes clear that Vern is alive in Finnell's memory mainly because he's been told so many vivid stories about this spiky character. In actuality the poet met him just once, as an infant. Then as the poem progresses it becomes evident that the poet knows almost nothing about Vern beyond speculation. He has conjured up a character quite vividly only to proceed to cast doubt on every detail he's imagined. And thus he sidles up to what seems his real intent, illustrating how every "I" is ultimately a mystery and alive mainly in imagination. Finnell's little conjuror's trick makes the real Uncle Vern both appear and vanish in one seamless narrative. The final stanza begins: "You are not at the track eating rib eye." The poem is not a portrait of Vern, but of his portraitist, who remains unsure of everything, sprinkling phrases like "I bet," "might be," and "my idea, not yours" throughout. This is a trick Finnell pulls over and over, book to book, speculating on the nature of identity and consciousness, casting doubt on how well we may know each other even as his imagery and music carry us along, happy to suspend our disbelief.

Once more I am reminded of Stevens, especially his closing tercet in "Tea at the Palaz of Hoon": "And there I found myself more truly and more strange." "The Fitzsimmons Fund" is far from Finnell's most complicated or ambitious poem, and it's not the best example of his wordplay, vaudevillian humor, or knack for phrasemaking. But it does illustrate how true and strange his playfulness can be, how much he relishes, to quote Frost again, "play for mortal stakes."

—David Graham

David Graham's most recent of seven poetry collections is *The Honey of Earth* (Terrapin Books, 2019). He co-edited (with Kate Sontag) the essay anthology *After Confession* and (with Tom Montag) *Local News,* poems on small town America. Now retired from teaching at Ripon College, he writes a column, Poetic License, for the online journal *Verse-Virtual.*

from
RED COTTAGE

Juniper Prize, University of Massachusetts Press, 1991

The Cloud of Unknowing

Took off on time, and over the Gold Coast
saw Lake Michigan evaporating
in veils of fog, and the fog similarly
ascending into clouds. We're in the clouds

now, United Flight 406, and a large man is consumed
by reciprocal trade, —"Our soybeans,
their labor!" Isn't electricity
running inside others, this animal fear

alternating with awe? We are flying
inside mother-of-pearl clouds, and our iced drinks
do not tremble. Big Jim is laughing
open-mouthed, silent, to what we hope

are a comedian's words inside his headphones.
Somewhere someone must be spinning a prayer wheel,
and we fly on into a cloud, a stately
pleasure dome. "What keeps us here?" the Khan asks.

Lake Michigan flashes sunlight from its face,
and a long ore boat pulls the widening
V of its wake, floating on nothing
but water, and all of the words for water.

Belladonna

Apparently, my people begin and end in Iowa,
with one Mary Keenan who suddenly
showed up in Council Bluffs, ready to scrub
the prairie from their duds and oak floors.

Beyond her, the tribe exists in a fog bank,
the clouds of paradise to some,
gruel to others. They are all anonymous,
except in a general Irish way, faceless

without the luxury of portraits handed down.
They mill around, waiting to shuffle this way
as Mary has, fog parting like parlor drapes,
her carpetbag shifted from hand to hand.

Packed inside are some heartbreaking things,
I just know, from the old country.
Name them, a general nostalgia commands.
They're heavy enough, heavy enough.

What I focus on, want to heft in my
real hands, are the potatoes hidden
in her bag, bound in rags like small mummies,
the eyes beginning to sprout. For her

they mean food, hope, or a last mercy stroke:
seed potatoes for the Iowa spring,
raw ones in winter if no floors need scrubbing,
or the lethal eyes if winter fails.

Never eat the eyes, my mother told me
as she peeled spuds, skins coiling
off like party streamers. I never have,
nor downed bleach with its skull and crossbones,

played chicken, my neck on the track,
or roulette with a real pistol.
I can't say if eating the eyes of potatoes
can kill, or how our family warning began.

Maybe with Mary's last winter, the last
parlor floor in Council Bluffs cleaned,
spring just a memory of chlorophyll,
and the plain potatoes, their eyes, mercy.

There is no work here, Mary. Go back
into whatever the fog is, to faces
more real to you than any descendant's here.
However stunning your face,

the flowers of potatoes, *Solanum tuberosum,*
might kill. It's wrong conjuring you,
beautiful lady. Give us peace,
a homely thing, mostly water and edible.

The Grand Burlesque

Somewhere here the women stripped and the comics
waited for laughs. Pasties
undulated in the carnal spotlight, and baggy pants
bumped and grinded. Over the expiring

punch lines, over the houselights blacking out on cued rim shots,
The Grand Theater loomed. What was that space for
if not our communal want?
The Grand stood there and took it, the swinging pendulum,

the city's medicine ball. In the liberated air
The National Museum of Bowling solidified, ferro-concrete,
windowless. We must pay to see the renowned tools
of the masters. Where comics

joked about Wun Hung Lo,
a champion's polished ball is exhibited, under glass.
Now we can laugh, a Rip Van Winkle laugh.
There's no commercial irony here, just chronic coincidence.

Once boys presented their fevered faces to the ticket booth.
Under age, lust aged us.
We paid extra for balcony seats, for intimate
eye contact with strippers exiting stage right, flashing

their G-strings, a vision, beatific.
A dollar more for balcony, our feelings luxuriously private.
A scattering of older men below,
their faces tilted back for revelation, and empty seats

for citizens who didn't need to see. Who needs
to recollect, anyhow? Whole faces, whole bodies,
are distilled. What remains is an emotional hangover.
The combo in the orchestra pit,

for example, as good as dead.
But the sax man's feigned indifferent tone, as though
desire were ennui, that's the pitch we take across the river,
and the drummer's tardy pedal work, the piano player's

progression of three blue chords. From balcony seats
we spied the comic in the wings.
His name, Muckin' Fuch, his plight, to stare at each stripper,
seeing each embodied verdict, every naked "no."

And what did we see in "The Dance of the Lover's Hands"?
Her hands were our hands, her orchestrated moaning
coming from the staged memory
of the watcher's flesh, from the pretense of hands.

A drum roll, a rim shot, and the houselights black out.
For nothing we will let you feel the lace netting
over her bed, the gauze between skin and voyeur,
between boys and a hard place.

Some Reasons for Everything

She cuts the eyes from potatoes
and feeds bucketfuls to the pigs.
He cleans out old mattresses
and stuffs them with fresh cotton.
She brushes the sorrel mare named May.
He climbs between the wheels of the boxcar.
Their gestures shape the air
between them into something else.
She gathers warm eggs in her skirt.
He spades up dark red beets.

Where they are the sky comes down
to their feet and onto their backs.
They shuffle along, kicking up dust,
and feel the sky between their fingers.
Between them are numbers of miles,
several counties, a few towns,
and the three-headed god
of seeds, of soil, of chance.
With their hands they pat the air
into the notion of a child.

Because she believes in God
I will sneeze three times on Tuesday.
Because he picks his teeth with a matchstick
I will believe in God.
Her tying a ribbon in my sister's hair
will persuade me love is needed.
His weeping at the kitchen table
will give me bitter encouragement.
Because they shared a blackened room
for a split second and loved
one another with their bodies,
my first word was *light*.

Taking Leave of St. Louis

Nota: man is the intelligence of his soil,
The sovereign ghost....
Nota: his soil is man's intelligence.
That's better. That's worth crossing seas to find.

—Wallace Stevens

1.

Smoke used to rise in any shape we wanted,
llama, mountain, neighbor girl, even the sleeping
face of a grandfather. We felt kites pull,
but little how smoke took refuge up there,
suburb of clouds. It falls over our homecoming,
odor calling up a factory at blank heat,
red bandana and neck, a man's pupils, pinpricks.

If it had color, this odor would be the brown
vein of the Mississippi. Just a breath or two
drives sorrow to our feet. The few remaining
tenement homes, spray-painted confessions
down front stoops, tiny yards where dust rises
up as funnels the size of children, these will not
walk away. And Spring? It's a curse to alley weeds.

Cousin, show your heart, from the same orchard
as mine. Let's plan to forget these windows
boarded pitifully up and look ahead
where we're driving. The bridge's legs built
stone on bedrock hold us up out of grace,
don't they? And the spans arching us prove
people did, and we must, alter our stories,

so gaze as far into water the shade of our city
as the river allows. What inches under us
with a prehistoric moan if the ear is turned right
is no patriarch. It lies there, the weary giant
offspring of rain and of mud giving way.
This bridge feeds us to the metal arch curving

pain into understanding. James, people made
this rainbow, even the elevator rocking us
inside its leg, and the room at the top shaped
as cut onyx where it's hard to walk, and downturned
windows where our faces are meant to show.

The Old Cathedral: a toy of distance.
A high-rise window is rectangled sunlight.
Something is forgotten there. Bad relations?
In the middle of the city a man is falling.

2.

Once, I did live near orchards, peach and
apple and pear. I drove gravel
roads alone spring nights bordered by
trees laid out in grids. The orchard keepers'

clapboard houses sat stories above the bowed
limbs, and like ether
light went out their windows onto the arching
flowered limbs, seeped inside them,

then gone. How they got there I pictured as
immigration, clans speaking a cross of old
and new tongues and walking oxen under loads
over the Sawatch, down Debeque Canyon

to there, the valley opening as old words,
kept. Oxen pulled to lather
wagonloads of saplings readied to go into
their quincunx, roots bound in burlapped

globes of the old dirt, the finger-size
trunks of peach and pear and apple tagged
Prunus persica, or *Pyrus,* both
communis and *malus.* Wise and faithless

as a beast I drove orchards, white moths
hectic in my headlights from tree
to blossoming tree. Whose winters but mine
coerced me to see moths as parts of flowers,

migrating orchard to orchard in the common
will to be fruitful. I would halt
between two orchards, switch engine and lights
off to let trees and moths back inside

their darkness. And to let me picture
myself as cave salamander, eyes withered
to nubs, organs visible past
transparent flesh, who with touch alone

must know where the world ends, I begin.

3.

A man is falling in the middle of the city.
It might be bad to say once more that he stretches
his limbs in air, has a yawn on his face.
Bad as a child who won't let the thing alone.

His eyes, wide open now, are taking in the earth
below him, and us, too easy to forget.
Gravity is not love. His eyes, bluish, the pupils
constricted black into which stars and nothing go.

I'm tired of cause and effect. James, let us
retell his story, one like an arch, a bridge
growing out of pain to justice. Pears withered.
He walked absent-mindedly out the window.

And I want to walk off as refugee, with a tidy
bundle of goods balanced on my head.
Then he never will fall as the newspapers said.
The right sound makes the possible necessary?

You may be right, cousin. As he falls his sleeves
ruffle in the wind he makes. Are witnesses
accomplices?
                    Or else he stays

rooted in air, a tree in the sky, untethered kite,
a blanched face. If you call him your uncle
he must come down, and we must drive through a city
as through a being that was once our body.

One Hundred and Fifty Springs in Hannibal

That Spring the teenagers filled the sandbags,
as was the custom, then built the levee
as tall as their shoulders. Mothers raised
their babies overhead for a first look,
and said *River* and said *Wall of Sand.*

The flagpole sitter kept his winter promise,
one day in a shack on a tower
for each town year. He grew a civil beard,
squeezed out a waltz on a concertina.
Fathers in parlors cultivated the old tongues.

The river, he would not rise. Dogs whelped
from our husbandry, irises flourished.
The flood that we built the wall to survive
showed up downriver in the Bootheel.
And we, the townspeople, walked the dry levee,

the band playing dance tunes in the square,
two or three of us touching the wall
as mourners, to forgive, put their fingers
into names in stone, a woman in a bonnet
handing out red poppies, free and real.

That April the chills came over the old man—
a Mr. Taylor—downstairs. He tapped
his ceiling with a broom handle-
Send down some heat. He blamed the river,
he blamed me, as though my winters were in him.

And that May a woman brushed out the blonde
tint in her hair. She sat at her dresser,
mean to herself, working the brown
roots out, speaking of her alias, her eyes
blacked out in photos, the platinum bouffant.

The flagpole sitter climbed down in June.
As the flood we needed failed
the town went into its history at last.

The Gulf of Mexico took in our years.
New dogs napped on porches in a first July.

Summer came in cicadas. My bride watched
a neighbor shoulder a catfish up
the alley of smells and silence. It had jaws
to take young turtles, birds tired of flight,
eggs dropped from the bridge by a boy.

On the Lookout for Neighbors

We, the feeble, sit alone on the lookout for winter.
Our best windows clouded with breath, our wills
dormant as snails, is it not hard labor recalling
leaves jostled in the sycamore? "O daddy not
that again," my daughter might say if I had one.

If I had one I would tell her, But it's January!
The sycamore is again an old self, a stick of a god
aborigines drew in their cavern. The bark peels
back in the white of baby teeth. Child in me says
bootprints in snow circling the tree are my neighbors'.

It says a mother and daughter trudged out in snow,
just because. The daughter did make believe
the sycamore was the statue of the lady you climb in,
saying the right words. And the mother? She did
neigh and stomp in snow as the pony for her daughter,

all a bad lie. No daughter waved from a make-believe
statue's crown, and no mother neighed on all fours in snow.
Two boys left the prints in snow. Out my window I
watched them circle the sycamore, firing silent and new
air rifles into an old nest, finding no sparrows.

Father, where are our neighbors if not with the tree?
I can't say, Amelia. All we hear beyond our wall
is the ocean that talks in the shell, that static
from the ones who disappeared. No single voice from
mother or daughter sets our littlest bones to quiver.

Our neighbors, gone. Long ago in distance and black
good stories make up, a star left her six sisters,
overworked father, mother pretty as clouds.   Why,
father? Some say family troubles, her electric charm.
Now we see it as we must. I would not picture it.

Everybody's Business

A moth called their window into being.

It spread day-old wings and pressed the shriveled
grub of its body against the pane,
holding what had passed for air in place.

Their windows could have housed dressed manikins.
Life-sized panes faced the little courtyard,
hardly a courtyard, of trash bins, an iron table,
one chair. Night came an hour earlier there;
day, in metallic clamor followed by whiffs
of yesterday's stew, arrived before real dawn.

It was a night after a day like any other.
They sat, and sit, with rigid backs offered
as souvenirs, heads bowed in the vain act
of eating. Silverware is clinking, never to be
crossed on plates. Grains of salt are falling

that man and that woman will not let fall.
They shy away from memory. Sure, his sideburn
is curly and her chin nondescript, but bona fide
legs are missing. Maybe windows compromise us,
fingers of intimacy framed to look public.
Glass is solid. Beneath the windowsill
is more her weakness needs him to admire.

It's lethal seeing through things. Air is mortal,
the moth may suffer, windows can melt back
to histories. Facts can do those people in.
It's not enough to say *ear* and *chin, elbow* and *hand.*
When the story is good, salt falls on its own,
a cheek rises, and a forearm twists in its skin.

The dead remain dead. Everybody else must go on
thinking up biographies. Those two draw curtains
for the night to take hold so the four-legged ones
can make their courtyard rounds. Andrew rubs shyness
out of her back, the fear of-immortality,
her backbone a snake, Marie, shedding white skin.

Little Cloud of Dust

So many really interesting professions
now open to us, from soup to nuts, from game theory
to grace analysis. In the get-up of childhood
you shot a pigeon, testing the tenderness in the feathered
world, whether a Casper-like ghost with wings
would steam up, and how many BBs would make you wise.
Some of us scrambled ants in a skillet, young
Mr. Wizard's tasting iron and piss,
sprinkling the skeletons in roses for bees.

Today I'm the nirvana for eggs
and carry around like in a money belt an old game.
Walk in the dirt, a stone to your eye, investing
the dust with a miniature city, with people too small
to play house with. Watch the stone fall
through the imagined stratosphere, until it kicks up
a little cloud of dust. Your target blown to smithereens,
it's a milk run. Missed, and you're shot down
again, a smoking comet, and you die, a little.

Was this my game, my genius, or something in the air?
Men inside a mountain wear it around
their mature waists. Old playmates of ours, shot down over
dirt and make-believe cities, they rose up
to see a toy world mapped in light on screens,
and to listen for an empire's thundering horses.

Red Cottage

You know how it is.
Your accident lets you meet a long-lost friend,
one whose love meant the world to you.
What's coincidence
but a slender awareness of merged parallels,
a thing you suspect goes on all the time.
Harmony, a kiss, a word you savor on your tongue,
all striving toward the horizon,
toward that depot.

Well, imagine how I feel.
Tolstoy died in a red cottage.
I am renting a red cottage!
Now I occasionally look toward the snowy woods
for Sophia wringing her hands,
that woman held at arm's length from her husband, dying.
But all this is bullshit.
I live in a red cottage
between a ridge named after an eager animal,
and a river called by some Breath of the North.

Wouldn't you feel once in a while
that what surrounds you
is the makings for a folktale,
a legend, a story to bring children up by,
then doubt as they grow body hair, their voices changing?
And so I feel haloed by this stammering white air,
blizzard, the black shawled mourners in the woods
nothing more than hungry wild fowl,
and a hateful man dead who put blood and bread together.

Over Voice of America

Some nights the quiet is all wrong. A tape,
it plays white noise. These nights I crown
myself in earphones and tune the short-wave in
to new music of the sphere. Grandmother voice
over Radio Albania wants to send over a hit
about wheat, and love. Over *Voice of America*
our voice is simply enunciated as if only
foreigners have ears. Silence is a drawn chord.
Between Tirane and Washington the static is
a Geiger counter gone sane. I tune the BBC.
The Repulsive Aliens play their catchy music—
codas from the white dwarf before collapse.

Some evenings I haunt my office. Windows open
out to Mary Lyon's grave and campus maples
kept pretty by will. The hour we love between
dog and wolf comes as stars show up, up there
all along. In my dark office I drink coffee
I cannot see, start to disappear. I make up
faces for students blasting maples and her grave
with Culture Club, The Police. Hair is green,
cheeks flour white. Mary Lyon said, "Testify!"
Dickinson took a carriage over the Holyoke Range
to her own seminary of despair, a dress
kept white in legend and a whiter sustenance.

More white than crystals Parker melted in spoons,
a hero addicted to pain. Students here know
Stalin's white Siberia and each red cent doctors
earn in their cures. They know Reggie Jackson,
Patton. Bird is black, fiendish, jazz-like.
Modifiers are right and wrong. Bird did burn
his room in a colored L.A. hotel, yelled Fire,
colored and naked. He did die in a baroness's
Manhattan suite, laughing at Dorsey on T.V.
Don't those stories kill? From L.A. to New York,
from fire to laughter, he played hopeless rooms
we can inhabit because he did not need hope.

Bird lived, died, lives some more. The last time
I visited Dickinson's grave, it was occupied.
Inside the black iron fence young lovers lay
clothed on her grave. He was on her and on her.
I have not yet been back. Friends, make sense
of those lovers. Were they mocking the virgin
in legend, she who knew Babylon inside out?
Tell me in some nights a Parker solo hums
also out of you, or a Dickinson phrase
moves your lips, cryptically. Our ears record
sounds of dead stars. Tell me we call them back
since they call us and we can hear, once again.

The Isle of Lepers

Once more someone has set fire to the foothills,
little mountains of scrub pine, of Fords
shuttled up dry creek beds and left for better
or worse. Once more a long island of smoke

waits overhead. I can call it The Isle of Lepers,
then simply look back down. No, island,
you did not come from seasoned leaves and a boy
who helped them on to air and ashes. Now

some things this March are unwilling to burn.
Here in Tennessee I know some poor white
is to blame for smoke, for me naming it The Isle
of Lepers and for naming him Jody, The Redneck.

My sky in sickness draws out my own sick wisdom—
The one called Jody kneels. With his thumbnail
he strikes a wood match. Now a pine goes up.
I make him trudge the dry creek, leaving his Ford.

Once more someone has set fire to the foothills,
contorted limbs of redbud, cars abandoned
after joy rides, a tortoise bearing a burden,
creatures from the three worlds. Their new selves

spiral up to the island of smoke. I am alone.
Down here I am left to look up to the island
home for ones of fear, to try to forget Jody,
the one I thought up and who thought up the island.

Down here the young man I was will not forget me
in the poverty of fear, burning letters that shamed
one of two lovers, my lightning war, mine,
words going to smoke and dirt, words expiring.

Singing Tree

When all your flaws become a point of view,
when your limitations let you hold what's out there
in your palms and get to know it well,
when nothing can improve the sky with its mountain ranges,
castles along a river bluff, and the sound of a bronze celesta

then maybe you'll walk out dumb one day
under a blossoming tree, who at an old distance—
from your window, say, smudged with winter fingerprints—
looked yellow-green and almost sick
with Spring, and see, hear, and smell a queen

who again must pass out the petals of her largesse,
tiny as the eyelids of sparrows,
and who suckles at her hundred breasts
creatures who moan, chant, and then fly off
to a city where their sweetness is bartered for a song.

In the Stars

Last night and tonight I've kept an eye out
for the half-dozen stars you named
The Hurt Woman. In the house shadow
tossed by the streetlamp I've tried to stand
unmoving as one of those stones circling
the field on the island. But you know,
the head starts to soon tremble, angled up
at the salt-flecked continent between
one star-bear and a hero. And it's hard to see
past the civil lights of streetlamps guarding
our domiciles and the flimsy matches
struck for a smoke with a nightcap.
They go up and fuse in a corona
over the city, and they water down
the constellations I don't know on sight.

Know what I think? If The Hurt Woman is
up there healing in the black sanatorium,
you drew lines to six stars and jotted up
a woman from the stolid lights.
Don't get me wrong: you're no god,
unless children pencilling in their bestiaries
dot to dot are gods. In your eyes
she was the wounded one borne on a litter
down the black mountain, the hungry stars
the old ones saw as beasts kept at bay.

In my eyes another hurt woman does not heal,
pale thing, nebula, embryonic light
the ancients named ether. If I were sleepwalking
she'd be beckoning me with salt hands,
Save me, save me, down the echoing corridor
at the end of touch. I'm just a freak,
she'd confess, a freak, and she did not heal.
Our boss found her, her room tidy as
Ptolemy's sky, the ceiling resting on her eyes.

Where is your sky and where The Hurt Woman?
Not over our heads, not in the stars
pinning the suffering ones to a black vault.
Your sky is interior, a nervous system,
and The Hurt Woman must be burning you
as she heals in the justice of a new sky.

Altar Boys

St. Gregory the Great's peeling white spire
is a snapshot, now, leafed in
the organist's hymnbook to save the old
house of worship. Two decades ago

and more I paced off the miracle distance
between communion rail and the wooden
pews for the meek, waiting. And was paid
two crisp ones and worldly months

in absolution to don the black and white,
light the dark cakes of incense,
and walk around the heavier-than-human caskets,
keeping the living from the dead.

How much will you pay me to forget
the heft of black cassock, the starched
white surplice, the weight of
a boy's vestments and a gilded censer?

A penny? A penny for each of memory's
unblinking eyes to pay the limping
ferryman to pole me across the smoking
river to forget this side?

Even there Father O'Keefe's grudging Requiem
douses the puttied flesh into
Abraham's bosom. And there boys recollect
the cortege of black limos parting

Fords to the roadside for the silent hearse.
Our absolution is days off in the hell
of forgetfulness, so we remember,
we altar boys, the luxuries of serving

the dead, the jumpseats facing backward
inside Caddies, green awnings floating
as at lawn parties, the fresh
greenbacks tucked in our fists for good work.

We did little but were young. To be the only
messengers the bereaved could afford
we spoke into our hands, our awaited Amen
flying after O'Keefe's plain Rest in Peace.

And Sundays in flannel suits, small fedoras,
we dropped into the passing basket
envelopes of change, envelopes depicting a church
of wood, our names embossed in the corners.

Swimming at Night

The water is still and warm. A stillness
that my weakness calls peace, a warmth
the old human in me says is mammalian,
still harboring salt. If I step into this,
wavelets will break off from me as my name does,
paged out in the air terminal. Like the static
of the first explosion that is doing in
the everlasting. The little stars are twinkling.
The sun for months has borne down. It alone
has cracked the clay about the pool's border.
It has heated up what I think the dirt desires,
water. Miraculous kudzu and young cedars
just outside the redwood-stained fence are coming
this way, toward the pool where only the benign
outlasts the maintenance man and algaecide.
It is a summer night, air full of exhalations,
and warm and the water warmer. No one tonight
will sense me floating naked and blue
from the water lit up and colored by the one
underwater lamp and the pool's blue walls.
What flourishes outside my body? In darkness
all distance is the same. The kudzu out there
is as close as my clothes prostrate on concrete
over there, as close as the snapshot of himself
the visitor buried in the powder of the moon,
coming and going in peace. In a pool shaped
as some vital organ, some mammoth's or one
pulled out of a forsaken constellation, I float
in the heat of the mammal and lose touch
in complete touch. I will float on my back
a few minutes, watching the dark space inside Orion,
feeling pity for nothing, neither clay
nor desire, for I am warm, in love and lethal,
accomplice in the night and the stars' witness.

The Great Bear over Grand Junction, Colorado

That summer I noted the calf's bones
turning whiter in the unadulterated sun so
coolly I could have been a second Grand Mesa
or outer space. Indifferent air worked
the russet hide away and showed the white
jail of ribs. My friend still used
whiskey to feel something, even pain,
in temples and eyes as if that stinging shot
with blood meant joy was out there.
He was fat. At our factory he worked
himself into an ignoble sweat near the plastics
oven. His name was George, that's all I
can remember. He sang Hank Williams and limericks.
Evenings we walked the irrigation canals and
sat under cottonwoods to watch dusk
lay down its silk over that spent water.
Before the breeze went up the mountains it made
leaves wave like a village bidding so long.
We drank potboilers and watched idling
mallards show how water flowed around
them to the Gulf of Baja. Once a coyote
walked past on the other bank without
sensing, and once George pointed to the Great
Bear and said, *that used to be me.*
There were two times at the canal, dusk
laying silk down flat on the water and
water always inching under it. It
must be good enough to quit the Earth
once and lie spread-eagle in the heavens
for us to get our bearings, and good enough
for bones to bleach in sunlight after
the body ends its pain, and not good
enough that summer to stay here always.

Pass It On

—for Robert Stewart

I'm trying to piece together one river from the river-feelings
stewing on the back burner. It's like
reconstituting any old memory. Just add water, since we're mostly water.
That acquaintance you made time with, her whole face
is in soft focus, but her duck-like ambling
remains, and her dear ignorance of it. And another thing: "the benign."

Maybe there is just one, the way every downpour is still
the first rain, for it's always falling pitchforks
somewhere, the way each emotion is the last. This river was just
another Ozark stream on the lookout
for potential flotsam. You and I had city in graffiti
all over us, learned in the frontier thesis: put walls up
against wild innocence, erect the dwellings and christen the metropolis
Possum Trot, then hang the nude called Kitty over the bar, the Great
American Desert in the parlor, passing it on, these beauties
we sweated through, mastering.
So we weren't seduced by the Big Piney's come-hither clarity.
No, not much. And pigs fly. (Once a cabbie
whipped out pictures of "Ocelot" from his goose-down vest.
She was in mink sprawled across a Caddie's hood, and the man said,
     "Man, check it out. A hundred." Her eyes

were suckholes.) There were stones on the bottom looking up at us.
I believe we paddled over them, believe
we canoed on into our charted fears and the real rush
we had driven miles to inherit, adrenaline
doing its job, the mapped boulders at their stations.
And it felt good.
                    What's left of anything
but hard-boiled eggs pickled in jars, the cool mind housing
the old hot facts. I think there is a world out there,
and a woman nursing a beer at the Do Drop Inn.
She's not Mother Nature, this beast of beauty, not anymore.

from
BELOVÈD BEAST

Contemporary Poetry Series, University of Georgia Press, 1995

Headless Horseman

I come from St. Louis. This may explain this tic I have
Of squinting, at any hour of the day or night,
As if asking, "Is that Katrina Van Tassel
Getting on the bus to Sleepy Hollow?"
Then again I am the namesake of the patron saint of Paris,
Who cradled his head like a baby in his hands down from Montmartre.
He carried it into his grave, resting in peace with it, at last.

St. Louisans put faith in their eyes—within reason
And a couple blocks—and we citizens,
To a child, don't trust the graph paper world of Descartes.
Thus, we have perfected the famous "rolling stop"
At intersections, looking both ways, then both ways again.

We do hand it to René, however, when it comes to doubt.
We could in his honor add under the fleur-de-lis
That graces our city's flag, *Cogito Cogito.*

It's not that we break down weeping and publicly
Confess every little pyramid scheme to some local newshound
In some Borgesian Garden of Forking Paths,
No. It's just that we've studied the history of *adieu,*
Which boils down to fifteenth-century out-of-the-body travel
Through the vehicle of perspective, from which we catch sight
Of the head of John the Baptist, belittled,
Horrified at his own martyrdom. It's on a platter for Herod's Feast.
Salome is nowhere to be seen, unless
That splotch with its back to us is her.

We've studied good-byes
In streets that radiate in a stilled
Explosion, that all along promise us a sun at
The center, a kind of geopolitical model of the Big Bang.

What's more, St. Louis doesn't end at eye level.
It goes on to an underworld of catacombs where good solid burghers
Took picks and dug out subterranean
Biergartens as their neighborhood grottoes. St. Louis summers

Went on stewing overhead, smudging the sunset, sentencing
The less fortunate up above to try sleeping in bathtubs.

It's just that each of us remembers a long, hot ride
In a rocking streetcar, growing seasick
Riding downtown, a thousand miles from saltwater,
And remembers resting a head (which kept saying *I'm going dark*)
On mama's lap, and keeping our fingers crossed that being
Grown up was not being seasick, except at sea.
Imagine our surprise, growing up.

Years pass. A man ends up in a stick house,
Surrounded by snow-capped mountains, which demand a lot of attention.
It has come to this. The mountains are his pupils,
And the first lesson is this: he resides on 27 Road,
Just twenty-one one-hundredths of a mile north of H Road.
I don't know if I'm going to like
This teacher, says Grand Mesa, looking down
Into the green grid of the valley, at a pictograph of a house.

This man writes down what he swears is the winning number,
And scrawls a map to Shangri-La, all in ball-point
On a niece's hand, which the man squeezes
Tightly, for safekeeping (and maybe just a little good luck?).
The little girl draws his portrait, and he
Kisses her on the forehead for it, puts it away in a book.

Years pass. Things fall out, such as hair.
Each winter keeps plowing more furrows in the brow.
A book opens, of course, a portrait falls out.
It is and is not his head, there on the Big Chief paper,
Which, itself, is a haircloth of slivers, and filaments from rags.

Oh, you're not going to like this face, I tell my old friend Brom Bones
From Sleepy Hollow. *Let me have a minute with it alone.*

Give a little girl a pen (which is tantamount to
Plucking a feather from Cupid's wing, then handing it back)
And she'll draw a picture of her uncle's potato face
Without a neck, none at all. The hair will be a ragged afterthought,
A ruse for the skull, against its awful confrontation with space.

A handful of whiskers dotted and dashed in on the chin, and full
Lips, slightly crooked in the embryonic stage of smugness.
Ragged mustache, attached to the nostrils by a thread.
And the eyes, behind what look like
Glasses held together at the bridge with black electrical tape,
My right eye in a perfect, effortless wink, without one wrinkle,
And the left one wide open, like that Egyptian hieroglyph for our hard
    r sound.

Years pass. I was born in St. Louis. Little did we know
How dark we would go, how even the grottoes
To the Virgin in blue, upended bathtubs, and the neighborhood watches
And corn boils, the new chains of burger joints and the feasts to John
Would do little but spray our souls with bad words in Day-Glo.
You didn't know about the piece of sky ahead of time,
Did you, the one your fiancé would bring down on your head,
Even though the city ordinance clearly called for everyone
To look both ways first. But you'd occasionally raise a little *H*
When a scheme for justice would fall out and crack and ooze
All over the soapbox. Some system. Some egg.
You would grow up with a big pie-face, as if
Long ago with The Bookcliffs peering over your shoulder
You drew your future self-portrait, drawing mine.
Maybe people do this all the time, ignoring
It, claiming it's a coincidence when at the intersection
They run into their biological moms. Don't tell me
What's become of the map on your palm, or the winning number.
Imagine their surprise. The song says we still got a long way to go.

On the Taconic Parkway at Nine Partners' Road

Straight ahead looms the ghost called the Catskills,
Aloof, homogenized to a blue-gray by distance
Where Rip is catching forty winks
In the petting zoo, as children touch his long beard
And jerk their hands back, worried it might come alive.

If a storm is itself and a soapbox oration
Belittling our life and love, if silver lightning
Scrawled its insignia on the slate of the Catskills this instant,
If that agent called Thunder then came, I would believe
Small, jovial men were at nine pins in the mountains once again,
But believe it only within the realm of my car.

You understand, your face is over my shoulder
And there are too many true stories about turning around
To see just once more—a face, a city in flames—
And someone gets turned to salt, to stone, or is exiled
In the underworld, after which someone else is torn limb from limb
Along the Mediterranean, these tales repeated for ages.

Most of the world goes on without us
And sometimes right through us, in x rays of our faces
Or as infrared images of illegals,
And only much later do we discover how they harm us.

Today's radio will tell of a marital disturbance
With a neighbor turning to discover
The cause of gunshots, and being damned herself
As the abode of the shades of the dead,
Seeing her friends that way.

As for me, it's a two-day soliloquy
Beyond mountains and great lakes, through Babylon
With its pork bellies and corn futures,
To a room where my back will be kept to you.

Invasions of Privacies

Soon the local dove will stop its five note song.
Its throat will cool, and its wings will ease to its sides.
Soon a shadow will part from its host in the hour
Between the bird and the moth.

Hours like these give us pet names for use in the dark.
Honey. Peaches. And someone holds a finger and a thumb
To her lips and whistles, *Time to come home.*
Hours such as these drop

Gauze over the neighborhood. Now it might be wrong
To see the fat boy in blue running shorts
Kicking the little blue spruce, or wrong to smell barbecued ribs
Between the Finches' and the Millers'.

A drive in the car does no good. The light mothers all.
In the back seat of a cab a face from the Neanderthal
Is lit as Alexander's. Light graces every hitchhiker.
Isn't that B, an old buddy?

Isn't that gray kitten by the road an old pet called Midnight?
This light only publishes the past.
Even a lawn's plastic deer tells how dusk is a mule
Bred from the night and the day.

Staying home is ignorant. A June bug pounds at the door,
Needing a witness. It will just roll over on its back.
Ugly wind chimes and horselaughs and shouts for Billy
Make themselves right at home.

So in this hour break and enter the crossbred light.
After all, dusk hangs the private
Lives of neighbors in the air as if they're out to dry.
Step into dusk. Take them down.

This is the egg of what will be. See how the gauze posts A
At her window, her hands clenched at her throat?
Covet her. Wonder if she gestures from need or from fear.
Midnight and noon, come home.

Grotto

Just through the winding circuit of three-storied mansions,
Just playing deaf to the echoes hailing us
From the walled estates, reminding us of who we really are,
Just being a little more patient and we shall see
The lake, a seam of darker blue through the trees.

Then it's simply the stairs zigzagging
Down the bluff face and we're there, where the lake
Breathes in a way, more sedate than the Atlantic
But out there the horizon is nevertheless water against sky.

A man sits on a wrought-iron bench, shirttails
Out and a two-day growth on his face.
Each bench features a brass plaque with a donor's name
Etched in a gothic manner
And we who sit here see things partly in their names.

The man is not myself, we are very different men.
He watches a woman I will call Venus
Sunning herself alone, oiled, turning more happily brown
And as she rolls on her back as in bed
She is unable to hide a flaw, and he feels closer.

Late summer bees are lingering, exploring
Openings with odors, and some colors—
The wooden trash bins and a soda can,
My mouth, and I notice the flyaway hair of Venus.

Each of us needs a small, empty place
Lined with sea shells
Where his next breath comes from.

The cooling towers of the Zion Power Plant
Stand the beach just north, and I think of castles
Of the future, all in rubble—like Dunstanburgh in Scotland
Apparently dead before it could reach the North Sea.

When Venus notices his looking
He turns to the white cursors of the sailboats
(One of which I know is called *Miss America*)

And soon looks again at her darkening body.

The tops of a few Chicago skyscrapers
Peer over the lake's horizon miles and miles away,
Rising, flooded, no one will say.

Cupola

Most of the world here is as invisible now
As your small, raspberry beauty mark
So what's left but the day's cupboard of images
And tomorrow's promised deliveries, the rumble
Of a commuter train speeding along the lake shore,
The ambient voice of the lake forever asking, *Kiss?*

The stairs squeak, it is dark.
It's like climbing up into a community head,
And more—being able to peer out
As though from gems bejeweling a head
And seeing things, even backwards
So that finally we have eyes in the back of our head.

There should be pigeons here, there should be feathers
And guano on a hay-strewn floor,
But this is also home for the Night idea
That up here a person is the squared and plumb locus
For whatever needs to rise,
This cupola, abbreviated steeple for lay believers.

Are there walls around you? Is there speech?
In darkness, are all distances the same?
Is at least part of you emptying itself
Into the night, like a pitcher being poured on the moon,
And the dark side of the moon at that?

Maybe it's just me, but up here
It's a real job with few perks to surmise
That everyone down below is asleep,
That the sleep of most will be rich and blemished.
It's a job to pass their nocturnal work along,
Another sandbag for the bleeding wall
Standing against the Zuider Zee.

So please grant one a bird in the hand
That is simply a bird in the hand,
Grant another swimming privileges
And another sex like it used to be

And still another that a son not fall in the jungle gym
And still others for an apartment without insects,
For an eternal struggle, for the hair of Rapunzel,
For the next buoyant word, for a tree or a picture of a tree,
For a stairway down tonight,
You on the landing, my eyes in your hands.

Kiss

Most of us believe Lake Michigan will win
Its long, nearly breathless seduction of Chicago.

In a new oral tradition Cupid will be all abuzz,
Whispering inside the ear of Adler Planetarium,
"Let the lake have you," and Eros
Will walk Shedd Aquarium to the long bed of sand.

Then stars will lie down with fish
In a peaceable kingdom inside the lake—

But that's eternity we're talking, not this morning
As the Lake Shore Limited hustled us along
Between the lake on the left, the city on the right
With its high rises looking
Quarried, hewn into something human, dragged
Shoreward and propped there, brooding lakeward.

Even the Art Institute was a talisman
Meant to ward off the lake, but giving shelter as well
To four hundred photographs telling the story
Of fixing shadows, and people paid their respects,
Shuffling the maze of walls of pictures, and nodding.

In your favorite one a couple is kissing.
The city goes past them in a blurred pant leg
And in unseeing faces under a beret,
Behind eyeglasses, under a postwar hairdo,
In a trenchcoated man with hands held behind him
As he makes his constitutional, in the curved
Rim of the sidewalk table whose job is to gleam.

In the background City Hall is a ghost of itself,
Unfocused, peering over their heads
So parentally there should be a story about it talking,
Saying, *Ah, to be young again, to have a real face,*
Remembering itself when it was water and stone.

They are kissing, and her hand is entranced, hanging—
Not exactly lifeless at her side, but as though

Life had been summoned urgently elsewhere.
They are kissing, and his hand is forming an 0
With thumb, forefinger. They are kissing,
And their mouths are the still, quick, molten center.

In our long kiss, which one of us is city,
Which one of us is lake?

The Generic Manifesto

Today, Sunday, September 10, 199_,
Ensconced in the form-fitting chairs of the Burger King
That spies across at the Edens Mall, now deserted
Because of a Blue Law (which is a forced,
Silent march to the hymn "If It's Good Enough for God,...")

And lonesome as American Sundays are lonesome,
Where the six-day-wonder-of-a-world
We love, finger, and put on our gold cards is exiled
To the Monastery of Memory, or to Monday's Theme Park,

We hereby declare "The Generic Manifesto"—
Not that there's anyone else here, just my Whopper and me.

Everything looks like something else,
And today it's that other thing that concerns and awes us.

New, unruined buildings hunker down along the strip
Like a gauntlet of ungilded bunkers—
A layer of concrete or a metallic fascia imitating cement,
Then a layer of tinted glass that intimidates
Us, reflecting our own failure at seeing,

Flatters us with our darker, brother images,
Gives us the willies, as if each
Internal compass were jammed, quivering like a water witch,
And we are up to here in Anywhere, U.S.A.,
But not that town guarded by righteous row crops
Where Bowser, knowing citizens by footfall,
Lifted his toy mongrel head to bark at a select few.

Now here is so interchangeable with there
That homonyms are endangered, that this is a kind of paradise
(Or is it "pair of dice"?) where a pit bull
Is barking, attacking something pitiable.

We're just becoming godlike, provided
God is vague, everywhere—like the plasma
Brooding inside and over our major cities, speaking of which,

Go ahead, stand our cities on their heads (as someone
Close to me has concluded of women) and they all
Look the same. A _____ is a _____.

So please don't alarm self at disorientation
As you peer into the other's horizontal face on the pillow.
It is always the morning after the night before,

And that queasy stomach and wide-eyed
Ignorance at where you are, and what you did, and with whom—
Hell's bells, we all feel that way.
It's the Hall of Versailles Syndrome, all
Those mirrors generating subjects from one king.

We, the undersigned, therefore believe
Meat and potatoes are our bread and butter
And as we bring home the bacon
We shall be drawn down the strip and past
Structures and green vegetation and one firmament,
Drawn by a formerly horizontal face pictured
Standing vertical in the doorway, beautiful—
But then again, whose face shall not be?

Rapunzel, Rapunzel

You could feel your way to Lake Michigan.
You could play blind, touching each estate's wall
As you step through Lake Forest to the bluff,
The designer beach below, and water
Kept so comfortable, in civilized waves,
That drowning would be joining the best club.

It's not that villagers here carry clubs,
Or see better than you, to Michigan.
They're just protecting the sheen in the waves
In the hair of their daughters, behind walls,
Hair pouring over the girls' shoulders like water
Preserved in strands, draped over a bluff.

Don't misread their blank surfaces. It's no bluff,
Those clean, wordless walls to a rumored club
So private its code name sounds like water.
Feel along the walls toward Lake Michigan
And you may end up in it, period, end of wall—
Unless dumb luck in the shape of a wave

Spits you back on the beach. Then you could wave
Off the big lifeguard and stare at the bluff
Where like a golden ladder down a wall
A girl's long, blonde hair descends. You'd feel clubbed,
Spit up like that by Lake Michigan,
And then hair like spun gold let down to water.

Then Life would have some choice: crawl in water
To Wisconsin and beach yourself as a wave,
Or climb from the beach at Lake Michigan,
Hauling your hefty self up the private bluff
Using a girl's long, blonde hair. At the club
The smart money says you'll climb it, like a wall,

Since you can't swim. You're up against a wall.
What's worse? Lake Michigan's cruel water
Below you beating driftwood into clubs,

Or the scissors to which the hair with the waves
Leads you. You could trace the hair from the bluff
To the crime scene facing Lake Michigan—

Your name scratched in a wall, a Scotch and water
And a golf club with your prints, and the bluff
Lit up by a golden wave breaking in Lake Michigan.

Hannibal, Revisited

What if I told you the Mississippi is a joke of a river now,
That the silver bridge that would hum a mile-wide
Note with us and with the Impala's bald tires, it's now all oxidized,
That Huck and Nigger Jim work the inclined streets,
Mouthing their rap for chump change, and carving toy rafts,
That no one was auctioned here, that Hannibal is a nonsense word?

Could you then spot the new me as I walk head-on
Into a fence that is whitewashed daily, and see the enlarged
Eyes of Hannibalians watching me bump into their solid, blank world?
Their eyes ask point-blank, "Where are you from?"
I may as well say, "The other side of the moon."

Order a man to just try eking out a life here
Some years ago in four dirt-cheap, connected rooms,
Let the rooms articulate with one another like a four-word
Imperative sentence: *Live; sleep; work; eat.*
And you have the makings of a house of bricks,
And against it a man scratching his back, waiting for the bus
To talk him across the Mississippi, to look back at a rusting bridge.

But give that same man a piece of luck
That he bends over to pick up because it flashes on the sidewalk,
Do that, and someone like you steps out of a cloud and breathes
And revises our rooms from command to declaration: *We live and sleep
    and...*

And so today there are as many Hannibals as there are eyes,
Most, but not all, tricks with smoke, with mirrors,
Buildings, shoulders dreamed up out of something burning, something
    flashing,
That turn out pretty real when you walk into them.

Today black people walk in our rooms on 6th Street
Where once, out of sadness, I pinned your wrists down with my knees.
Do they walk through the ghosts of us in our old rooms,
Sleep on us, eat sitting on our laps?
And don't we ache from them, this nostalgia, this home-pain?

The man in the window scowls down at me, across the street,
And I should answer, somehow, but my heart is a jar of smoke.
Instead I turn on my heel and begin limping off
In a kind of three-legged race
Into the present, toward a silence that is a mile wide and brown.

Say something so I know where you are.

Ballade, U.S.A.

—after one of Villon's "poems in slang"

In a city who is my mother a John Doe turns less white
He hangs from a metal tree   He shows how gravity works   How the
    world turns
He's been pruned   He's been grafted
By angels who sweet-talk pain   They make it flower
The wind muscles in from the Mississippi   It frisks and loots him
But he's blooming up there   He's the black rose
Put your hand in your shirt   Make a fist   You know what to do
Neighbors have thumbs   They have forefingers disappeared—
"Now count to ten   Now covet somebody's purse"—
Beaten in our name   Beaten in the name of strength

Say it's real dark   Say you're looking for Someone Small   Someone
    Rich
Rent a child's eye at the corner to spot angels
Don't wear white   Don't use your name   Don't even smell
Somebody might say   "Meet this lady   Meet Ms. Uzzi"
And you'd lie down for her   You'd be your own effigy incarnate
Say it's real dark   Say you're jogging in Forest Park
Remember Big Questions   But don't forget the Bigger Questioners
Angels who can alter you   We're talking forever
Your outstretched arms   They won't match
Beaten in our name   Beaten in the name of strength

They'll cuff you behind your back   Guard each curse with your teeth
You'll curl up in your mother of a room   Don't even think
Of yourself as clothes   Think of your body as dirt   As in "burial park"
An angel might hang you out to dry
And time is going to be going very fast in your back
Bent over   Worn down by the glacier
Don't dream   Don't give your fears or your loves that right
You might do two things at once—Sleep and speak in the ears of angels
You might pay them a tongue   Yours   Mine   Your lover's   A
    stranger's
Beaten in our name   Beaten in the name of strength

Sir   Words escape between teeth
When angels look the other way   Take a nap   Sometimes just blink
And spit gleaming on a chin   Sweat glistening on a forehead   They're
    prayers
Against a tree   Against a knock on a door   For a glass of milk
Beaten in our name   Beaten in the name of strength

Acmeist

The steppe is prose. It refuses to turn back
On itself, the way a child's rolling hoop will, or Venus or Mars.
It turns back on itself the way a wolf does, or a nation.
The grasses come up past a train's wheels and whisper the new facts
    of life,
No use genuflecting here. You can't eat us.
From the boxcar Acmeist Mandelstam sends his eyes on a courier's
    mission,
Twenty, fifty, a billion *versts* to Siberia's end, a bungled horizon,
A smudged draft of the first imperative sentence.

Between the slats his two eyes, his nicotine-yellowed fingers holding on,
Are punctuation: *Quote, period, period, unquote.*
Two eyes that report a yellow oval, blue-black wings, there! in the bones
    of a birch.
His third eye identifies it: *Goldfinch.*
His fourth eye is cocksure—it's Anton Chekhov inside his rented *tarantass,*
A goldfinch in a cage jolting along on unsprung wheels going to question
    Siberia.
The Acmeist puts a hand out through the squinting slats,
Turns it palm up, offering millet seeds to goldfinch Chekhov.

He recollects Chekhov's words: *"Before Lake Baikal it's all prose."*
And for the Acmeist, Lake Baikal is the liquidation
Of the steppe, its back turned on its earthen history at the smudged
    horizon,
It is the ice-cold saga of empire, with a sky of goldfinches flying
In and out of cages on buoys, singing the glories of the Kremlin
    mountaineer!
Lake Baikal was Wednesday, will be Friday, is never Thursday.
A bird has its wings clipped in mid-flight, in mid-song, and is falling
All day Thursday through the verses of Lake Baikal.

In Vladivostok he catches up with his eyes.
They interrogate *him,* from fish soup, from puddles, from the dregs
Of birch bark in his tin cup, and the agent who stands in his ear
    commands,
Don't eat what's in your wooden bowl, it's Lake Baikal. It's poison.

So the Acmeist makes believe he is the labor camp's scarecrow,
    eating garbage.
He turns to look back at his nation, nipping at his heels.
His eyes—two periods between which his lines have been excised.
His future reader is in his mouth, *like* a goldfinch.

Our Epictetus

We depend on things that if put on cassette
Or videotape, or even written out in plain English,
And then played back later at home
With enough quiet, and maybe a cool drink,
Would seem insubstantial to build our lives on.

If you wrote down "air" or "foot,"
Or took a snapshot of your eating utensils,
Then wrapped it up like a present, later opening it
Alone in your bedroom, you might be spooked
At how your life is so...well, very, very menial,
And you might call somebody, even anonymously.

The ambient noise is our friend.
When it ruptures and the sirens materialize,
Or the whispers materialize for spare coins or shoes,
I, for one, feel let down by our friend,
Who is a wall of noise, albeit a wall of silk noise,
Letting the barbarians rip through.

It's like this: mouths have been grafted
On army blankets, on cardboard
Domiciles about the size of children's playhouses
That are squatters on the sidewalks,
From which pleas are hurled at us, as if
Anyone's life is snippets
Of pain, hawked on the street corner.

This is why I wonder about Epictetus,
For whom an empire was a vast diamond of an argument
For sensation, where pleasure and pain
Were whipped into making their daily rounds,
Where his master twisted his leg, passing time.

Didn't he arrive at his own blue law,
Following a road of sorrow, no son of a god himself,
To where the world led and ended at the Forum?

Now all these mouths are uttering his
I told you it would break.

The Irish Wilderness

Tonight I sit up with Ursa Major, telling him the story
Of the cultured pearl of our loneliness.

The eighteen-wheelers in this rest stop idle like dozing animals,
The kind that sleep, eyes wide, standing up in the pasture,
And each trucker, coiled up asleep in his cab,
Is the genii of his truck, dead tired.

The sky wants my head, of course,
In its maw, between a pair of twinkling canines.

Who, after all, understands desire's tongue
Of sibilants and fricatives, much less speaks it, if not
The one standing in her distant grotto of common sea shells,
Feeding a sparrow in her outstretched palm?

The one whose skin I love chafing against mine, whose soul
Is the blue-headed flame of a pilot light,
Has looked at me, more than once, the way a small cloud will,
And said, "Explain that one more time."

Long ago one Father Hogan on his mule into these Ozarks
Led a clan of Irish families, homesteaders
Pulling on their handcarts the Old World's carcasses
Of children and seed potatoes into the New World.

Now locals call it The Irish Wilderness, that plateau
Of limestone and scrub oak and freshwater springs mumbling insanely,
And today in broad daylight I hiked into it,
The chert gravel under my boots, coerced to speak,
Reciting its few choice consonants, and I repeat them for you two,
Great Bear who will eat me, woman with her tongue in my mouth:

One morning they disappeared, just like that,
Like a bowl of water in August, a plate of millet for sparrows,
They disappeared without trace, without logic,
The sustenance of the wilderness, an enactment of faith,

And today in broad daylight I hiked into it,
As I rounded a stand of scrub oak and their knotted gargoyles,
And I nearly disturbed the flock of vultures
Forming a black rose around a dead thing,

And you who house your tongue in my mouth
Don't see the beautiful wound.

Rapunzel, Again

What I recall is a boil of voices at my back,
And a big, deliberate step down under the tavern's electric lantern
(That looked a little like a pumpkin with a candle in it)
And a plan in my head to walk back to my room
With my eyes closed, feeling my way along the walled estates.

My shoes echoed off the walls. The night air was rich
With the odors of mown lawns, and something curried lingering.
Behind the walls there must have been roses named for daughters.

The night itself was a velvet curtain
That she parted and walked through, bringing her face.
It teetered, I remember, floating in the night, like a lotus or a buoy.

She began saying something, looking into
My chest, as though behind my shirt was my real face, and asking
The powers there to show her how to "cut off her neck,"
To help her lie down across the commuter tracks.

She carried a pillow under her arm, a ring of keys in her hand.
No, you don't want to do that, I said once I really heard.

Her hair was platinum, and short and spiked.
To all my questions she said no, or asked for my help,
All the while looking into my shirt pocket or buttons or pen.

Do you have friends? Can I call someone? What's your name?
Do you live nearby? Can I walk you home?

My eyes wavered between her face and the pillow under her arm.
Please help me cut off my neck, I don't know how.

I showed her my back, walked home along the walls, exonerated.

Tongue. The End of the World Is Roadless. Exile

The Danube has a mouth. Out of it the tongues
      Of Europe pour in a polyglot stream,
And the Friendly Sea is the continent's black thesaurus.
      Near the mouth I live in a noun,
Exile, with stick walls for consonants,
      My own mouth open round as a vowel.
I have a name, and in Rome my old friends excuse
      Themselves, bringing it up in public.
A new coin says in Latin and with the Emperor's
      Face, it's year xxxvii of Augustus.
To get to the end of the world I could not march
      On a stone road radiating from Rome,
Worn smooth by the Legions. To get to this town
      Called Tomis (named after a man
Butchered here by his wife) I paced Rome's un-
      Forgettable streets weeks on the ship's deck,
On legs I ended up naming *taedium* and *terror.*
      I kept my back to home, to avoid my wife's
Face on the sea's wake. I offered her my back.
      And from the wooden Nereid of a bowsprit
I looked into the three Seas and vomited
      To their accompaniment, even into
The *pax* of the Bosporus and the friendly Black Sea,
      Even my ration of Rome's hard bread
Exiled. The end is one large mouth and a score
      Of smaller ones, none speaking the mother
Tongue. The end of the world is roadless. *Exile*
      Means I hold my face and walk around
Inside the stockade, displaying it like
      A baby held up at eye level—
Look, my face is wailing, it is innocent.
      Nevertheless, the minutes parade by
Like Legions, and the natives treat me like a dog
      They know, seeing it gnaw itself,
And let be. *Exile* means the red-haired
      Girl I have put lips on me and breathe

As I sit on the riverbank, I call *Erato,*
      After the muse. *Inspire me now,*
Beauty, betrayer. It means my ears thirst
      For Latin, that the native tongue is dice
And the clack of dice, that with my own tongue
      Nowhere, every unheard word of Latin
Is an ideal world, a stillborn Atlantis.
      Out here, I am Rome.
I wear the skins of animals just like
      A native and run helter-skelter inside
The stockade, dodging the barbarians' poisoned arrows—
      Taedium, terror, taedium, terror.
What I do with my stick walls and open
      Mouth is write epistles in verse,
Tristia, and send each year a book
      Of these "Sorrows" to Rome. What I do is
What the red-haired girl does, posing
      As letters of the alphabet. Her mouth
Opens for *O.* Legs spread for *V.* I grow erect for *I.*
      Most air is liberated as it expires
At my mouth, and it walks off, sometimes limping.
      It will walk up to the sky and say
Nothing. The air going into *Tristia* for Rome
      Wears a long white toga. It lies
Face-down at the feet of the First Citizen Augustus.
      This air says everything. It says,
I was wrong. Forgive me my dirty
      Book about love. Please at least ship
Me where our tongue is spoken, where
      An ear exists for my mouth. My real
Crime was to imagine love. My real sentence
      Is to imagine Rome here by the
Danube's mouth. Out here, I am Rome.
      My alphabet turns its head, gazing
Back at me, a vowel in a bearskin. Inside some
      Sticks I push a bowl of ink
Nearer a candle. The stockade is an *O* around
      Me, an *O* on a page of the steppe.

My friend in Rome wears my likeness in gold
      On his finger, my friend holds it to his ear—
Believe Pythagoras. The soul follows the body,
      Haunts its place of rest. I am
The steppe and the river delta, I am the Friendly Sea.
      The months melted away like sherbets.

Real Poetik

Once I helped decipher a writer's posthumous papers. Before that
He had been a perfect stranger to me, except as I
Had caught sight of his putting one word in front of the other in *Knock on
      any Door,*
His novel of, by, "The Proletariat." That's mean to say,
I know, a kind of lie, because his book was Chicago with a bay window
In it, and something very much like a man sitting in that window at a loss
      for words,
Whose mouth opened wide against the *El,* whereupon I
Screamed. His posthumous papers were the usual dead writer stuff—drafts
Of flawed masterpieces, the imperfections red-lined
And the new, improved revisions careted in, also in red, all
Looking like an illustrated bestiary, and versions
Of versions of stories, mostly of his own ambitiously herded life
As he walked his body up Mount Rainier, down Chicago's tenement
Alleys, rife with raw, metallic echoes and razor-sharp knowledge—
I've walked all this way to fear. "Posthumous papers"—sounds like the bills
And letters and junk mail breeding in the mailbox after death,
Doesn't it? Or the *Times* and the *Shopper's Bulletin* stacking up in front of
      the door,
Or his passport with his last photo coming too late, all
Because no one had been told the belovèd had died. Anyway, I'm squeezed
Into this TWA wide-body and I'm
Here to tell you the belovèd is dead. Long live the belovèd.
I think I'm flying. I may still be over California. I'm not alone.
My ears hurt, and there are hundreds of us facing east here,
As if for a sunrise service, when the belovèd will greet us at the airport.
I think we're heading to the center of the country where all the Belts
Meet—Rust, Corn, Bible, Goiter, in one vast cummerbund.
In derelict factories in Gary and East St. Louis the new corn cults meet.
Do they ever stop to think one moment about
The belovèd, jailed long ago and far away in East Thermopolis,
Wyoming. He put down his bedroll too near the town's belovèd hot spring.
It was winter. He was one cold colored man, a cinder in the snowman's eye.
There were no coins to jingle in his pocket, and his life and bad fortune
      were illegal.
He got thirty days. The cult members can find it all in his
Posthumous papers. It's all on toilet paper from the jail, in a neat script

As tiny, condensed as a colony of ants. These days
A man might write just any old thing down on an airline's paper drink
    napkins,
Because he's bushed. Let's see, it's 3:08 am inside a wide-body.
The air coming out of the little overhead nozzles is telling us all
To take a nap, be good, shut up. *Pssst. Pssst.*
But Seattle's lights must be burning down below, out our port windows,
In a sky as dark, as stimulating as coffee, and someone like me
Must say, *Seattle's lights are burning. They were a kind of ark into which
Our eves went, two by two.* And so it was that last night
A wide-body climbed up through Seattle's dark, low ceiling,
I *think.* (What's memory but negotiations
Between management and yesterday over who did what to whom,
And when, or settlement talks between this moment hissing from the air
    nozzles
At 3:09 am and its spouse over childhood's custody.) I left Seattle.
There was no sky. It was exiled for winter. No problem. In lieu of a winter
Sky were artificial lights on buildings and islands, on rusting fishing boats
And undulating on black Puget Sound, duplicating the fake sky.
I left Seattle, left a heroine inside the city's self-made night sky.
She changed into her freedom suit treading water, holding her breath in
    the middle
Of a river, stepped barefoot on the riverbank, writing her name in mud.
    She said
That at the end of the line one must turn, or write homilies.
That fear at the end of the line is the gardener, cultivating the next breath.
That without a real sky we tell our own fortunes in the city's lights,
In earthbound constellations, the blue tongue of a lit match here,
A flashlight beam there casting a stranger into his own bust,
Headlights turning the corner home, the sidewalk, then the front door
Lit up, an island ferry in scratchings of light, the ferry's lights
Gossiping on the surface of Puget Sound, a few lights that must mean
Something big on Bainbridge Island, the rhomboid of a curtained window
    flickering
From TV light, the pinholes in skyscrapers, a Mickey Mouse
Nightlight. I left Seattle. From the wide-body it was burning. A city is
Its own sky anymore, with a fortune to be told at eye-level,
With mortar and lit filaments. It's 3: 11 am inside
A wide-body. The air comes out of the nozzles overhead in homilies.
Silence is good. Naps are good. Patience is heroic. Think of the fir trees

Of Seattle, their convention of stoics. But we who barnstorm for beeswax
Earn our red eyes, must spit it out that last week
Was Seattle, Minneapolis the week before, Detroit before that, and that
Next week is St. Louis, that a month is four cities, then *home.*
That's our calendar, with no picture of some Mount Rainier in alpenglow
As he was last night below us, out our port window.
He was smiling, his head of snow presented on a platter of clouds. He
     smirked,
He saw the white lies down the Pacific Coast waiting for us at L.A.
And not just its ganglia of lit cars, to and fro in exurbia
Under the air's gauze, not just the palm tree at the airport at its forced
Labor, standing in a big pot, orienting us, saying, *Welcome.*
To Los Angeles. Look, I'm a palm tree, see? Where you guys from?!
Not just the vending machine in the airport that would dish out espresso.
What's a mountain for if not to see for us? Mount Rainier smirked
Because he saw the blue tongue of the TWA agent tying
The truth in knots—*Your flight will be delayed briefly to St. Louis.*
Mount Rainier was glowing, seeing the airport lounge closed, the TV
Turned off, no heroic Letterman to save us, no
Espresso left in the machine. California closed, the belovèd nowhere.
We proles slept sitting up, we proles on the floor, prole
Heads on baggage, on another's prole shoulder, just a colony of bigger-
Than-life ants. What's a mountain for if not to see for us proles?
It's 3:13 am aboard a wide-body. T-
WA has given us drinks, free movies. A man might
Write any old thing on a paper napkin. The big woman at my elbow
Watches without earphones Bogart as Nick knocking on doors, to redden
Her eyes. He's going to fry, but I won't spoil her surprise.
All of us aliens here face east, posted in orbit at forty thousand
Feet, hurrying our pairs of red eyes into morning, goosing the speed
Of sound, beyond which even a declaration like *I love*
You is percussive, a Saturday night special saying *Die bas-*
Tard. So in the syntax of powered flight, we are imperative: fly. But if
Lift fails, if the verb of the engine dies, or the subject (you understood) has
A heart attack, we are incoherent, a sentence fragment, mouths open
Falling all over the U.S. of A. Underneath the port wing
Eight miles of liberty, then the constellation of some city.
It looks like a burning strand of the national DNA, it looks like a homily
On fire. At my elbow she cries big tears as Nick is belted

Into the chair. All the gossip on the El is he'll break down
Like a baby. Get to know any light and it grows eyes, opposed fingers and
    thumbs,
It breaks out of the bestiary. We aliens know a few stars
By name—one calls herself Madeline—and we are as kites to them,
Tethered to down there, the string and the message we are passed along
Friend to friend, star to star, across the U.S. of A.
The big woman is done crying and leans her heavy head against the port
Window. The world out there is just beginning to show up again,
A little pink giving the clouds bodies. *Mount Rushmore,*
She thinks, *or just some cloud thing with four or five heads, maybe more....*
Nick is dead, long live the belovèd, long live the beast.

from
THE GAUGUIN ANSWER SHEET

Contemporary Poetry Series, University of Georgia Press, 2001

Some of you look into this, my mouth

A coin is a guess with somebody's face on it.

This penny flashing Lincoln's face,
then Lincoln's Memorial in mid-air
is a fatalist's stab in the dark, no matter
how it comes down on the back of my hand: heads, tails.

Whose in our indivisible nation
is more legal tender, its face of dirty copper,
my freckled one? However the coin descends

I must walk it off, must walk
us through this, or the *e pluribus unum* behind its eyes—
behind ours—might get worn blank.
                                I must talk, even if I
mutter about a tongue, when the tongue itself
balks at the turnstile.

::

In our nation's capitol, the big marble of Lincoln
stares out over The Reflecting Pool.
The inverted obelisk floats on that shallow water, pointing down in a
    needle.
Day-in, day-out, he still stares into the pool, buying
its reflection from its master.
                        Go on, stare,
man-stone. Soon you'll be eaten
away by our lifestyle and touch—our fumes, our breath
along the Esplanade, the body's oils on our fingertips—

See, a father lifts his daughter up to touch
your monumental hand. She's scared to death, it's big as a cur.

We'll break you
down, we'll disappear your face, your old, gray, now-
marble eyes as large as apples. They'll survive,
souvenir eyes.

::

Some of you look into this, my mouth.
It's not the big door with lips opening to the funhouse.

What did you expect, a brass band
to strike up, a movie to roll
azure Tahitian mountains—
                    the fragrant
world, the delectable world,
as Gauguin would have it—
and gold Tahitian skins, their
                        searching animal odor,
a gilded child sleeping, a pleading turquoise
Tahitian goddess?

                Speech is half listening.
Another coin. I need all your help.
Together we can walk and talk, scoring
jargon into the tree trunks along our unblazed lives,
toward something like
an ocean. I need your ears.

Start our eyes

Let's take a few steps backward, letting it come
inside us and vice versa—but watch your step,

too far back and the soldiers in Manet's painting
will shout, "Damn your eyes!"
for bumping into them. Their squad is still shooting
after a century Emperor Maximilian
(part of him is a pale integer
subtracted from his own wall) in Manet's
own big painting facing Gauguin's.

Gauguin's picture is panoramic, our lives figured in
hieroglyphs, the colors compromised—he mixed them as he stood up
on two legs on Tahiti's soil, 1897—

We catch our breaths, we breathe out
in the same room with his fouled ceruleans, fouled
chrome yellows. The century's exhaust
has varnished them all: a lived-in paradise—

One meter seventy in height, he wrote back to France,
four meters fifty in width,
the two upper corners in chrome yellow, the inscription
in cursive on the left, my signature
balanced on the right, like
a fresco appliquéed on a...
                              chrome yellow
wall and damaged, peeling back to gold at the corners.

Back-to-back with Manet's soldiers
executing the Emperor, we make coins with two heads.

::

Gauguin's picture is a window
cut into the bedroom of our world.

Now our new neighbors answer
with skin, go half-naked, loom, just outside our window.

They're the picture of their young flesh.

They confront us, they conspire, picking
our apples and cutting roses, lounging bare-breasted
in the neighborhood. They moan, they mutter at all hours—
we are exiled from our skins.

We stand gawking, back-to-back with the firing squad,
lost about the best
place on the picture to start our eyes.
One of you says,
                    "It doesn't matter where
we start our eyes—with the mummy on the left
or on the right with the preoccupied
black dog, or even with the woman between them
picking provisional fruit...."

You (with those ears of yours) are right.

Let's compose it. Give me your back-talk, walking along
each personal cliff without too much fear,
our mouths open just wide enough.

Scratch, sniff

The world surrounds us, cohabiting with thought.
It's made of stuff, we rap our knuckles on it
for good luck, or we kick it, trying to refute it.
What's more, there's nothing between the stuff.

We wake to the world as if it were our pet
who brings in his mouth the day's news—
Morning fog. That 10 o'clock flight to D.C.
(time only to nod at Lincoln, whose giant hands
scared you as a kid) *You still have legs—*

Later our dog of a world takes as his cue
our miraculous reappearance at the end of our long day
to again bark and whine, to make a joyful noise:

We have been dead
and have arisen with the dog's help.

::

                              In Gauguin's picture, the head
                 half of the preoccupied black dog lies down,
                                      profiled, a good Sphinx.
                           He stares off beyond the gilt bodies
                                  to the centered white kittens.
                    The black dog's wagging appendage of tenderness
                        curls outside the picture, inside our world,
                              waiting for what we know of doggedness
                                to help the invisible wag, to help it be told.

::

One winter a woman and I conspired with ice.
Inside our rooms our breaths
were tissues of stuff, were counterparts
to the window's frost,
especially in her whispered "good morning."

To warm our souls we climbed Pine Nook Hill.
We built a snow monkey—more stuff,
more fluid turned solid: its stoic

face of cinder eyes, nose, and mouth
realized its fate: to dissolve
down the hill, then run unscreaming to the sea.

This same woman calls back that winter's black dog,
out of nowhere, out of the block of ice of then,
bounding through snow like a dolphin through an ocean
toward us, a monkey of snow, two people,

until we saw the signs—
tail wagging, his head full of teeth, bowed.

We kneeled.

        He licked our faces and hands.
We scratched his head. We rolled in the snow,
made angels, human and dog,
leaving our history in snow.

We aren't only ourselves, memory liquidates
even Gibraltar's experience, much less the cinders of Pine Nook Hill.

Scratch me, history begs.

::

                    The two girls in Gauguin's right foreground
                        stare out in conspiring question marks.
                Both keep their hands near their chins, heads cocked.
        Both gesture how lost words are, how this painted golden dirt of skin
                        on cheap canvas does not give our beginnings.
            Their bodies question sharing touch, they lean right, they ask,

                "What about my sleeping baby who knows no strife?
            Where do we come from? What are we? Where are we going?
            Isn't this the fragrant world, the delectable world, this living?
                    Isn't this forever, and always shall be?"

Come, endure

Each of us has had twenty-three homes.

We've migrated from the bed that orphans us
to the next cushioned chair that adopts our shape.
We trail the harvest of desire or necessity,
all because someone's eyes or our stomachs make us
take just one more step, or because a voice says,
"I can't live without you."

Soon we're up the ladder picking fruit
in one more Eden.

        We all come from St. Louis.
There the filthied Father of Waters we call the Mississippi
elbows his way through us,
through the circular city, our alma mater.
It makes a gigantic phi on the midwest,
neither alpha nor omega. It looks a lot like what it is,
an egg forever being fertilized.

Come closer. Just below cloud cover
the window passenger stiffening to final approach looking out sees
our houses materializing along the avenues, strung
like atoms along their helixes,

and closer yet to touch-down and a sigh
the window sees each house growing discrete
with a brick barbecue pit, a child's blue, round plastic pool,
an awning initialed "F," for example, or "Y,"
initials telling the sky, *Here we are.*

We keep descending until we finally touch
the long "I" of the landing strip. We get our motel.
We kill time until the late war news.
We take a cab to the window on Romaine Place
where our mother and father are about to do it.

::

Behind the bathroom door, the amber light
seeping underneath it like wax,
she puts on something special just for tonight.
She says, "You want me,
close your eyes until I touch you."

Who can refuse darkness
for her promise of flesh? he thinks,
but says, "Do what you
need to do," holding his hands over his eyes. "See,
no evil—but hurry."

She steps with no voice to the bed.
The vision of the sheet tented up by his prick
makes her say "o" and she sidles under
the sheet and reaches for it,
then screams, "What's happened to you?
It feels wrong, like a doll."

::

(At the window we mouth,

"Mom, dad, don't make me!
I will disappear on a Friday hunting a face in Waukegan.
Will get knocked up at fifteen to spite you. Will steal money
from your black pocketbook for pizza and Luckies—the clasp's
little assuring thunk of closure was a lie!
Will take drugs, will try slitting my wrist—
my life will be a family's influenza—
I will borrow your new Ford Galaxie for a joyride in a blizzard,
will fail summer school—'How can anyone fail summer school!'—
will move a continent away. Will not be
at your bedsides when you die.")

::

But he undrapes himself, his hard-on
under a tiny straw hat, fitted up like a village idiot,
a smile in mascara just under its crown.

"April fool's," he says.

"Who's the idiot?" she whispers.
"Take that stuff off, love me good."

Soon they are mouths, kissing—

::

(We at this window know their pleasure,
how touching is always
untouched, as if yesterday's caress left no residue.)—

::

Soon he unravels the sheet embracing her,
and seeing the unusual shouts, "What in the hell!"
to the black leather belt and lock she wears
guarding her pussy.

"April fool's yourself!"

Soon they aren't themselves,
soon are rolled into the be-all and path of pleasure,
and doing it, turn abstractly
into a vital oval and line in a seizure
until in their coming, all lovers come and endure.

::

Now turn from the window. Say to ourselves
"Go, now. Don't look back. Go."
Go back to some Morpheus Arms Motel,
back to the lure of painted bodies questioning us.

In time her body formed a "Y."
From it we entered the world, crying the new year in.

Out of mouths

Gauguin's two skeptical girls still cock their heads.
"But where do we come from?"

::

A coin is a guess
with someone's face on it, and whose on our indivisible globe
is more legal tender, your faces of Tahitian
dirt at the end of Gauguin's hand and brush, or my freckled one?

Your face is as good as mine.

::

Once, always
a boy sat teetering at a great height on a saddled pony for a portrait.
It was a pinto, and inside the boy America tended an urge,
to ride a horse named Silver into heaven.
He was too little to be human,
yet he had a nose on him, even then.
He smelled leather, and something like a dark,
dirt-floored shed covered with straw—"but it had four legs!"

He keeps the pony, he keeps the day's aroma
intact, sealed inside, as with amber.

Inside the aroma you'll find the day,
going about its business, an itinerant photographer
leading a spotted pony away
up a St. Louis hill, shaded by the doomed elms.

::

And so it is we come from eating dandelions
as kids, and from our mother
telling us we ate dandelions—and don't forget our silent hours, as she
would have it, playing
in the crib with a deck of cards

or the happenstance of our first words—*bonjour*
or *light* or *chocolate* or *papa.*
                    Even then
we told our own fortunes,
in numbered cards, in face cards scattered in a crib,
in sounds echoing ones from a grown-up's open mouth.

The world was a woman leaning over us.
It had a big mouth.

::

                    So how can you ask, "But where do we come from?"
            Aren't your days and nights now an egalitarian pond—or,
                        for that matter, a Tahitian lagoon—
            where the omnivore and 3:42 p.m. swim and crawl,
                    each keeping its eye on the other?

                        Which will eat which?

                    If you're so smart in your painted paradise,
        make something of the earmuffed landlady with ears buzzing,
                        cradling a shotgun at the door.
                    It's 1946, on Romaine Place, St. Louis.

                    Is she a permanent fixture, or 3:42 p.m.?
            Where does she this very minute swim or crawl?
                        Is she the omnivore?

::

We come out of the downturned mouth of an Uncle H,
the upturned mouth of an Aunt I,
hand in hand with the fable of the puppy
brought home in dad's peacoat pocket just for us.
It is a spotted mongrel to be named Daisy,
her stub of a tail wagging, the hole
in her throat growing.

::

Out of a father's mouth
fell Canada geese from the winter skies over St. Louis.
"It was night. Their wings must have been
coated with ice, or maybe they thought the wet boulevard
lit up was a pond or river—who knows?"
The drivers on Kingshighway screeched to a halt,
scurried, stuffing live geese in their car trunks,
St. Louisans out of a father's mouth, shaking their heads
in wonder— "pennies from heaven...hard times."

::

Out of mouths which would not eat us
we were regurgitated—
us, you, me—
and a stone wrapped in a blanket,
us, the world.

::

In hard times before St. Louis,
a young man bent over in the Nebraska Sandhills,
planting cedars against the everlasting zephyr.
He is our father, bent over sixty-plus years planting a seedling,
picking up a dusty coin. He stares at its face as at an answer—
he counts to ten. For a count of ten
he is masterless: free, in terror, as if the sand under his feet
were a boxing ring's tarpaulin,
and he lay akimbo there, masterless, free
or as if the sand under his feet were a trapdoor
and he fell ten days to China—
he palms the coin, planting it with the next cedar in the throat in sand
he makes with his middle finger.
Lincoln's face of copper will leach, casting
the cedar a little blue. It is one tree, it clutches a coin.
It will be as beautiful to father as Lincoln's face.

Out of hard times before St. Louis
we were ushered forth in grunts and moans,
St. Louis jerryrigged from hearsay in Nebraska—
"Sure, you'll find good work there," the hearsayers said,

"no more of this stuffing mattresses for Ace Bedding
in every god-awful shithole 'berg on the plains!"—
from headlines—"St. Louis Hothouse Gang Wins World Series!"—
from advertisements—"laborers, no experience, bring us your
broad backs."

::

From arrowed road signs to the future, from ads and headlines,
from hearsay, we were ushered forth.

Maps were money. Our mother and father were themselves
passed along by a stranger's word of mouth.
They were the stranger's secret.

From out of chapter and verse called Nebraska
they walked and talked,
from out of Spalding and Guide Rock, Cedar Falls, Superior.
From out of these towns they walked and talked.

From our mother's testimony, when "bread wasn't just given,
just like that," we were given legs.

She milked the family's lone cow on the hill,
a Nebraska milkmaid, circa '32.
She delivered it before school, her reddened fingers
quieting the bottles, for neighbors.
She scrubbed floors on all fours with a brush—
"like a good smart dog"—for a dollar a day.
She owned no Sunday stockings, wore red
circles on her knees, her eyes on the collection basket.

::

If a coin is a guess with someone's face on it,
now when we see a copper one
we think of our mother's reddened knees, those round beaten faces.
From her knee-testimony we walk and talk.

Out of our father's six-year odyssey
with the Ace Bedding Company, we amble, we mutter.
He wayfared the dustbowl towns in the canvas-covered bed

of a Dodge truck, a broken-down twentieth century prairie schooner,
sailing dustbowl farms, its abandonments.
He fixed sleep for strangers bone-tired for a decade,
purifying each mattress, a mummification,
"All for sheer pennies!" the advance man would disclaim.

Some pig farmer in Superior nicknamed him "the sandman."

His own sleeping-drenched face woke him
night after night to wonder, "What planet is this?"
He told the one-eyed great plains,
"My name is Noman."

::

And so it is we come from his cautionary tale:
A twelve-year-old boy whose labor it was to collect unserviceable horses—
the lame, the wheezing, the aged—sold to be
destroyed, lashed halter to tail, guided slowly through the dirt
streets of Superior, Nebraska, some parade
to the Great Northern's corrals, his own shirtless torso
dark as bottomlands along the Republican River,
a boy astride the lead horse, riding wordless to the cattle car.

Her kiss evaporates, his testimony calcifies

The two skeptical girls still cock their heads.
"But where do we come from?"

::

Remember the black dog out of nowhere
bounding through snow like a dolphin through an ocean?
"Scratch me," he begs. Do so, and he says, "We come from

unused diaries. A child-voice inside
a floating canning jar. 'Hello,
my name is Bill. I love to watch the clouds, I love to ride
my pony. She is brown like this river. Her name is Jo.
I live in heaven in Nebraska. Write me a letter'.
Love letters between one Wilhelm and one Flo.
Milk-ink summaries of love letters held over a flame:
'O, they'll burn, but they were on fire'.
A wadded-up list: 'soup', 'bones', 'dinner'.
A bill for 'one tire—
slightly used'. Illegible receipts,
the scratching like our father's signature,
near the end. An IOU (printed by hand on yellow legal) for three
dollars. A sky-written declaration of eternal love,
a sky-written proposal of marriage over the Nuckolls County
Fairgrounds, now a family of four-minus-two clouds.
A newspaper obituary wrapped around the
deceased's gold railroad watch. Inscriptions on watches
declaring feelings, most deep, eternally.
Newspaper clippings where their names first appear.
Official records sequestered
in the county courthouse basement, democratically
cached. Indictments. Suits. Manifests.
Sentencings. Postscripts. Salutations.
Newspapers where their names last appear."

Is the dog right, skeptical ones, you who love dogs yet doubt them?

::

From Grandmother F's face we also crawl.
It floats unavoidably near.
Her lips are trembling, and now our cheeks are iced
from her wet kisses. They are cold, evaporating this very day,
the cooling residue of once-warm flesh,
so that in winter we trudge through the afterlife of all kisses,
so that cold fingers are remnants of the air's affection.

::

To see her later stand behind the haze
of the screen door, inside the loose flowered dress,
forever waving good-bye at us, is to see

ourselves making history,
its search warrant, a charge lodged and dismissed,
grandmother hiding some booze in the pisspot, sliding it under the bed,
the Superior Nebraska Police confiscating it,
prima-facie evidence, to present whiskey and bedpan
before judge and jury, the whole truth unsaid.

Is the dog right, skeptical ones?

::

Grandfather F goes on to confess to the Feds.
The gruel thickens: "I bootlegged. I crossed state lines. I sped.
I drove like a wreck. I hauled booze from Chicago. I built secret tanks
for the water of life into the body of my black Chrysler."
He got parole after eighteen months, forever believing "only the dust
is free."

::

Her kiss evaporates, his testimony calcifies.
We are kissing bones, offspring.

It's his obituary surrounding the railroad watch,
its gold heft pushing down the palm toward the earth's core.
Grandfather F died outdoors on a kitchen chair
in the sparse shade of the neighbor's elm.

::

We stretch out in a hammock strung
between a tree trunk in the past and this very day.
The hammock forms a mouth, and we rest in it, as words
do on lips, as offspring do.

::

        We rest in the doughy, powdery face of Grandmother H.
           In lightning storms she stood, lights out, crossing
              herself, praying to "Sweet Mary, Mother of God."

        We step from between her perpetually clenched teeth.
                  She had no coin struck in her image.
                    She greeted fate with a grimace.
      Her voice was a musical saw, half lilting, half angry, saying,
           "I know he's dead-drunk in the alley, he's surely
           flat on his face." We sleep in our family gossip—

her secret first marriage to an Iowa bank robber, who failed
melodramatically, disappeared completely, taking with him
                    her only gold piece, hidden
      behind the picture of the Virgin above her bed.
      Did he, each time looking at its gold face, see hers?

One of you skeptics will say, "He spent it."
One of you skeptics will say, "She did."

Ultimata

The two skeptical girls still cock their heads.
"But where do we come from?"

::

A face is a guess
and whose is more tender, yours of Tahitian
dirt at Gauguin's hand, my freckled one?
My face is as good as yours.

::

We come from Grandfather H who was toothless,
looked like Popeye, and tossed us ceilingward
so we screamed to kingdom come, only to descend
to Dutch rubs, whiskers on our fair cheeks,
and our smallest toes screaming O! all the way home.

::

We are legends, and we come stepping out of legends.

::

He danced in St. Mary's Churchyard with a cross,
having acted as an angel in the transubstantiation
of a daughter's milking money into booze,
his lifelong changing of whiskey into piss,
all inside God's mansion.

::

We look out from another face, Great-grandfather S's,
as pious as a sunflower's.

It bows at the screen door,
in his hands the morning's prized gift of goat's milk,
as though all distilled whiteness
were held up in a pint milk bottle. "Oh, no!"
we did not say then, "not that stinking milk."

A photo of him, Wilhelm S, holding the reins of his pinto horse,
the Western hat with its brim rolled also in his hands,
the pin-pricks of his eyes saying,
                              "Look behind me
to the treeless truth of the Nebraska plains,
its ultimatum of a sky,
its hills forced down out of the blue—clouds
coerced into putting dirt on over their bodies."

::

                    We come from Great-grandmother S, who never died
                         in her barge of a bed but simply rested there,
                                   a giantess, forever, who never
                              dismissed her smell of damp mulch,
                         her storied life conjugated in her grandson's mouth—

                         "She traded horses. She was a horse trader.
                              She judged horseflesh. She'd put her nose
             right inside a horse's mouth to smell for sickness, you know?
                              She drove a Model T before she could vote,
                                   raised rooster tails on farm roads.
                                        Farmers' wives would say,
                              'Here comes that Minnie Hazelmeier S.'
                    I listened in lamplight with her to Del Rio on her radio.
                                   It ran on a car battery...."

::

From where do we come, when all these memory-seeds
do not germinate? From where, after the last mouth begins to quiver
bejeweled with spit, after our father's pig Susie
walks out of 1919 childhood into now's bedroom and begins to root?

From where do we come then, when the open mouth
then goes dry, when first-person fails?
Should we add a little water to documents,
reconstituting sheer avowals?

::

In Iowa Great-great-grandmother Mary K suddenly materialized.
At least pieces of paper imply it.
Mary is a Manila folder of dehydrated IOU's,
cursing us, blessing us. Why?
Because when we add our own juices to the Mary text
it's not exactly a Second Coming, is it?
Mary isn't a domestic again down on her knees, scrubbing floors again.
She has no knees. Dust is still king.

On the other hand maybe there's more to life than a corpse.
Stand Mary up in a forest clearing.
If she falls down and no one is around
does she make a sound? If so, did she mean to?

::

Yesterday I carried a dead wood thrush in a brown paper bag
to the woods' edge, dropped her there,
covered her up with the wet clenched maple leaves,
and caught a whiff of Great-grandmother S.
It flew into our porch window's everlastingness.
It left an asterisk of down on eighth-of-an-inch thick glass.
The shattered window scintillated as silica along an ocean.

Each second opens an ideal window through which we fly—
then we knock at lucidity.

::

This morning, no thrush song,
just the long *sh* of the zephyr through the trees, refuting the ideal.—

Conspirators, speaking

The wind refutes nothing. The two of us
vouch for it. As long as we can remember
it has gone about its business.
It makes waves in the lagoon out there.

The wind is nothing. It's just
an invisible mob.
Your distant relative is a dead bird.
Its song is the anthem of the mob.

Pardon us for interrupting. It's one of our jobs.
We are the pair of shadowy figures
behind the two skeptical girls, strolling toward the black dog.
The two girls made from dirty gold are our mothers.
The big shy one in front scratches her head
because our whispering is inside it.

We talk behind the world's
back. We debate
your lives. We take
our constitutional in your ears,
and you hear us, as you look in the mirror and ask,

"Who gave me this dishwater blonde hair?"
"Why am I so white?"
"What made me scream at Margaret?"
"Am I just instructions that can walk and talk?"
"When I say `yes,' who really means it?"

And in the mirror you don't move your lips to answer.
We are the ones strolling
in your head with whispers—

"Blame Grandma H for rolling
the dice, handing the dishwater blonde winnings on to me."
"Thank an island of clouds for my pigmentation."
"I screamed at her because I always scream."
"I am a walking, talking time bomb. No, I'm not. But then again...."

Somehow each of you go on living,
turn from your reflection, let out your breath
in a gesture of giving in to someone
who means a lot to you, is your health and wealth, really.

That exhalation fogging the mirror
before you put the coffee cup in the sink and go on to work
is our work. We two are that ad hoc committee
that never stops it talk about you.

Have you ever looked into a snapshot
where the old you looked back at you?
Maybe it was your birthday, and you tilt the cake
with its lit candles numbering your age so the future

can see your name in icing, can see how your world
loves you. You see a tiny moon of light waiting
in your eyes for the shutter to snap time's neck,
so the world can laugh, so you can pick at the icing.

Or you had a day to kill.
You take a bus into the countryside.
You smell cowshit, so you think of your grandmother,
who kept a milk cow and would hide the milking money
behind the picture of the Virgin above her bed,
so her man wouldn't convert it into the water of life, whiskey.

You feel guilty, having her big, round, white face conjured
this way, as if memory isn't the child
of your willfulness and at your ego's service, but kowtows
to something as low-life as smell.

Just so, the two of us are an odor and its host,
engaged in this paradise with keeping
a lethal forgetfulness at arm's length.
It's one of our jobs,

And so sometimes just smelling something
brings you your past, full of odd, nearly forgotten faces,
like Grandma's. They are wide-eyed in your window at you.
Smelling reorients you.

Just so, the two of us are disoriented.
We are like a woman and an old photo of the same woman.
We have peered so long this way into one another's
eyes we don't know

sometimes which of us is which. It's confusing,
like always just waking up but not enough to turn the alarm off,
this not being able to tell which one of us is
the dead one, which one alive.

We are lifers here. A heavy arm rests
on the other's shoulder. It's one of our jobs,
not just lugging this arm around,
although it's getting pretty old by now

but talking your life out,
then talking it out some more.
We are a dialogue in your head.
We are lifers here.

Aorta, keeping the whitecaps white

Today I mentally cut down the forest across the road
so we could see the last century.

She dawdled there on the bare, solidified wave of the hillside,
and we spied on her from behind
the tumbled stone wall, upright once more.

She was at the pump working the black cast-iron lever
up and down, making the rusty thing squeal
for mercy, and drawing up a pulsing
aorta of water into her own wooden scrub bucket.
On its side she'd incised *MK,* her initials.

::

If parents give us two genetic legs to stand on,
grandparents make us quadrupeds.
To hold one's face in both hands, to orient it
along a worn path to a single fathering face
is as good as walking to the moon, on one leg.

There's nothing wrong with being a spider,
having great-grandparents for legs.
It beats too much white space.

I am a spider. I am a millipede,
a thousand-legger undulant as an ocean, able to climb
upside-down, a herbivore Mary flicks off
the yellow squash blossom in the kitchen yard.

"Be off with you," she says. And we are.

Where everybody and his brother came from takes a long walk away
from Mary K, up a lichen-splotched stone wall,
on a thousand legs.

Night is coming soon,
hungry, able to see in the dark, covered in fur or feathers.
It may eat us, no matter how much we stand up, begging.

There's more where we came from, under
the palmate leaves we kick in the park.

It's dark now.
We're going to be some omnivore's dinner.
Or the morning lark's.

::

Mary has carried the evening's last yoke of scrub buckets
across her shoulders, into the master's big yellow house.

It was a stark interpretation she gave, of the goddess
with her scales of justice. And now
it's even more stark, for reason's nightmare
hands down its judgment:

"You have manufactured this woman
from a few vital statistics and some cold, stale hearsay.
She's a zombie.
I'm still one hungry nightmare."

Mary feels like a lead doll in her bed alone, living, breathing,
tuckered out, with the weight of the earth pressing
its back hard against her back.

She is barely awake.

Now she is dreaming
of no one but a doll of herself
down on her knees, scrubbing a floor
with a scrub brush with a mouth
that keeps saying "Our Fathers."

Soon enough the master's floor is the ocean.
Mary's job is to scrub it dawn to dusk, down on her knees,
keeping the whitecaps white,
the very ocean that rocked her here.

From
PIE 8

Bellday Poetry Prize, Bellday Press, 2012

Noise enters

   and is clothed in a shudder

A new thought has you
puts pants on the noise

It's a knocking on your door
come to save you

some spook
   unasked-for salvation

The guy's straw hat as Señor Astral
and the woman's mascara on one eye
giving a Nefertiti look

good to be saved

if only by questionable couples
     provided one

connects beauty with an eyelash
such an Egyptian

If she only walks or he has
a big ranch
   populated with odors

it will knock on your door

Who's there but yesteryear

Students sign their loans
so get smart
            money   be happy
America
            the little arguments next door
flared   magnesium
              burns a star

The trashcan marked Music Room S01
so inviting so
            to hide inside
would have been redundant
                 spell it

life
      radiate from and pierce
electrons   go through us

      we sense it not
            in any macro

on their way beyond any -ness

The voice
          the slight odor of trash
someone in a tight T-shirt

ram themselves through
                never
stopping   Why don't they stop

Tell why once a girl

cut my hair
        frayed   the decade ending
on the porch steps her fresh towel
around my shoulders
             my mountain pose loved then

my smallness
        The streetlamp stutter
traffic bringing its drone
              carrying
hush behind it
        Doppleresque
Lillian chatted planning a beauty harbor

My hair fell
dishwater blond then   now
        mess of no return
Wonder what I thought
        to the new world
to act the steps
        my being scissored

Dusk smells oily   the daylight
quits among odors and the rat

Call it day

Years Lillian
        working checkout at a
dark cleavage   her name

Hair grows hopeless

The season began inauspiciously

clouds part the coastal hills
tendril mist
     odor of iodine
          the barman's crossed arms
gull cries at your back
        the firs convening stoics
   in your scapulars winter
         begin a needling twinge

No other sign
Soon the night exile
            its storied constellations
a chapel lie
In its stead guide us
       tell us fables
fall over us mist and rain
rain and cosmic dust   dust and

night
     months before your cheeks appear
after a famous mountain
Randall works the bar
       his blues guitar

city lit here   pinholes
        some facets   others
during the rainy season
your eye shows up
    here   there

To return

To wake to cicadas again
insect palmists

To open a door
         August
all over you
         having missed you

Experience counts
afternoon feature   heat lightning
flushing the haze
        an anthropomorphic two
backlit
    then goners to words

Aging neighbors   yes brown grass thank God
Frigidaire

to suck on a screened porch
hidden in sweat   your animal

To whisper sweet on the deaf side

It's staring at it

and what's it called
                 not seeing

bad feelings   that brain tumor in him
then the letting go
              where was I Pittsburgh
Follow along if you
             want brushes against the skin
That's percussion
               small hammers on bones

Dad played his bones and won a tie
Vic Young Trader Santa Fe
                 in the soup too
up on the high pass   summer

in on from out of the air still snow thirst

Overdid the wise-acre

tallying up hiking fretting
overdoing it
back down the mountain

start lark
        Ascend thing feathered
with hollow bones to make
whistles of
        Started
soon he was here in oxygen depletion

die summit
        friends gather in an arrangement
dictated by mountain laurel
            and
a whistle the canine in him
            hear
take into his diaspora of odors on the wind
Smell oranges smelling him

But he's real
        a few cells
gasping for fluids
          The body's
an amazing patent
we made a ton off

the road up and the road down
any fool's
sins payable on demand
        at interest

Beauty dwarf pretty face

faraway hill
            shrinking down to us
we ambitious drives

please touch that face
with the back of tiny hands
doctors don't cure
        sick insurance men love

priests
        sins they keep
beauty   horizon
untouchable distant cows
view
        cool landscape

make us our
            lives call
us
            do or sleep or
and we're minor
fussing about the snowy

skirts   Excuse
know we be small
what to do in this cottage
you lapping up

her marvelous stew
                Wash our
dirty big dog
            If we touch her face
with our eyes then know
commotion in
        dense bodies

But one is on his way

this minute galloping
through
        villages fallen trees

a white regular
            a license to beauty

he's removed his glove to touch her
afraid we'll stay small

distant   untouchable

Accord

the sign at the border

road to one
            headlight
dividing mitosis
      is now in not in

another hoax of the apparent

creature at road's edge
            small dog in chain-mail
the chirruping
            coming
from a record of chirruping

This may not be OK
                  no armadillos no
            spring peepers
make the wind
      carry from a paper mill
rotting cabbages

make the drawl o
            complete stranger
o western boot o band
                  named Panhandle
play the Cherokee Lounge

Horton's Famous Bears

            flatter your hoaxes
the familiar dressed up
            in smells threaten the real
dance before
      dawn tomorrow in Broken Bow

A tube with lenses

mock
      the eye
burning in effigy
enlarged on
         the other side

Flock of vultures
      a black rose

orchestra playing in a crater

beautiful red blister

all I have and
        now
a coming
      through nothing pain
        bless
a pleasure circle   the pain

the nation round the offer

Here in you the shattered surrounds us

as ex does the memory of winter

NO HUNTING
                    the green crystals
and the old woods
        lesson of perspective

afterlife

hanging by a frayed rope
                swinging slightly

Here your dappled shade floats on grass
we bottom
      Green Emerald Lake our afterlife
sound of
A horse named you
            a young woman brushing it

Both go to the water wheel
turn in circles all day
pumping water
      that has fallen down

each sour apple

Whose future is white?

        the queue of icicles lengthening

Whose clepsydras drip into the bank

not one water clock
        so time and the glasswork sleeve

not separated at birth?

Your shoulder curved

under an eave a web with its larder

recognizable   quartered katydid
    one leg   one wing

You lie to you your mama's dogma quilt

the hissing thread cinches
    the tulip   the bee

for your thighs to Alleluia

just African snow Cape to aria

Ctesibius' bowls fill with Nile water

it's 11:10 AM

you-bird whistle
        you-puppet move

mold on the orange   citizen snow

If a nation

loving
        is somewhere

somewhere a hoe has meant
defeat of
            a feather

let someone sign
a neighbor

somewhere an alphabet
rises from tools
                walls

for the thing love

here gather round
cheering

&

        Everybody
between a mountain and a sea
your body is
            holy once

Mr Blue on the wall
                our write-in
Monday boils down to the earwig
Feel
        the growing
in a word probe

live   be a mall and a modest river
use the past perfect

Love dark

       love hot   who will kill you
the small tendons
strands made from weight
work   against the earth weight

white or   dark
the platter   lowered
    tilted toward the eyes

eat St Michael
       a bowl of ashes
pass me some ether
     s'il vous plait

that elbow

Captain white meat
steps   forward   sticks out his chest
Herr general pins the blue ribbon
flag of tenderness on the New World

under him
dark meat in
    calloused toes   bunions
his thighs hanging
     cock & balls
dark meat his   flexed buttocks

eat Adam   Eve after Eden
New   Salem
banquet be   us

The unterraced

file down to Lake Erie
they belong to
         what family army

the blind

August deepness as
rows hunker down
         the lake
could eat my car

         Erie's first
    isotherm invites its
second robs you
the third
    preserves
unperturbed blue

    Erie's fourth offers
    a glacial nightcap

remember   decades ago
There were weekends as big as
one family

    Mother Kyrie

mother grapes   round   first purple
    white patina of mold
    is table wine
the stained cork
abandoned on the floor

        is grapes   sibling seeds
knotted up   tiny flakes
of skin at the bottom of the wine glass

mother double   vision
        old world
New world legs going giving

under me
           a shouted Margaret leaping
a wall
      walking into a lake   mother is

a raw stomach next morning
asked if I wanted to see it

down the hall
where they took it out
                my mother's

Heaven stop here for sex

Just wait close
        your eyes and feel as though
the world in general   blowing
soul

       not like humping
miss thumb and one eye
unable to
       grip depth
Not like humping
     her past

much come is spilled
At one possible Eden
not
    enough   dirt in yr luv

This little creature

moving off on a hundred legs slides under the wall
Ain't it you
           seen   before

a few moments
your head
don't write down

gone pretty much forever

Here you go have
a cup of tea
it's made out of sticks

Feel good   all those bad
twisting you up
             a funnel of vines   get
digested   the alimentary canal
Let the canal take care of it

Bothers assume
          her face
    a pair of legs walk
through it   you   never

It's time

       the river
    brighter than the sky
the last thing   the light leaves

trees on the bank
        bent over
peering into
      floating debris
something upstream

    fallen

Facts
    abound sunsets
gone Dutch   treating us
crimson
      cumulus limned
over the Sunsick Hills
To take the sky
      really
the notion means   nothing
although members
add together
     and get premonitions

In darkness
    now   the shadow
of that large   rodent   mountain

To sit down on a tree stump

      to rest your elbows
on your knees
        your chin in your hands
A river must go away
once
     A stray dog never does
You point   your face
    at what
upstream given off
turning before
        your eyes
turn to the most
sullen god
a 40 watt-bulb behind
    a blanket
When the moon's
over
    a dog on an island
looks up even   as you dream
old enemy
    giving you
      a doubloon
To live on a stump
the light
       moving like silk rustling
Say nothing say nothing
back home
     you look across
a white farmhouse is standing
the necessary   strangers
You're all   aglow   say nothing

from
RUINS ASSEMBLING

Things to Come Poetry Prize, Shape&Nature Press, 2014

Light

It's beyond me, the pinhole in Hubble's eye tomorrow as predicted,
(and lingo beyond me—some chicken scratching,
a few noises standing up for red giants, string theory)

and Sol his own self making stuff take place, beyond me
the melting ice fern on the window,
these four lesions on my face, and yes a radish and maple syrup.

It's beyond me, the streetlamp out front of 3236 Rex Avenue
holding its sulfurous light over the street
and the cripple Debbie inside the post-war Cape
with her clenched hand.

Beyond me are light's eleven tongues,
the streetlamp talking her father's parked dump truck
safely through the night, and Debbie's squealing laughs
getting hit playing dodgeball.

Roger still tries to pry his sister's locked fingers
to show us the imperfection in Debbie's palm,
the reason for her crippled body, the meaning of life,
to which the streetlamp as good as says,
What is lit goes dark, what goes dark gets relit.

Debbie's fist will not open, especially now
after she's squealing lo these several decades,
even now after all this incandescence and fluorescence,
but in her palm I believe a dot lives,
like the still central point of a pinwheel nebula,
of a radish, of a rubber ball, a dot beyond me, yes,
beyond light. All it ever says is *Open.*

Mouth of truths

When I went back to childhood
I rode in the Suzuki down the street narrowed
by my greater self, past tinier post-war Capes
now closer, neighbors shadowing neighbors.

I resumed my nodding acquaintance
with the ghosts of fellow childhood children.
My niece chauffeured the Suzuki Sidekick,
slowing in front of 3241 Rex Avenue—
                              That's it,
my sister in the front seat growled between breaths
hooked to her oxygen,
                    That's it, with no
front door to knock at, no screen door to keep
houseflies out and let the breeze
come into it, just a dark opening into it.

I told my 47-year-old baby niece to go slow
so I could see the new neighbor mowing tall grass,
mowing Sharon whose face
I mocked for her pimples, whose perfect Sharon face
nods at the front of her head, so I could see
the other kids, recollecting
                    Marikos
smiling, his gyroscope balanced on a string,
Butch's big sister Diane teaching us chess
with winter's pawns, the Schmuck girls undressing
nightly in silhouette behind their curtain,
nameless black boy waiting in the honeysuckle
fort to play cowboys and Indians,
the hemophiliac Ricky and his beautiful sister,
both pale as sand, David of the overactive tear ducts

in our stay of execution.
Into the dark opening into it, our door-less doorway,
our neighborhood's mouth of truths, we put our hands, saying,
Memory gives eternity the mercy stroke

so we may leave Rex Avenue in the Suzuki,
the heads of childhood rising soap bubbles,
our hands still attached at our wrists.

Father of the man

The Child is father of the Man. —Wordsworth

It's Sunday, April 2nd. Just yesterday a bluebird
was thought to be seen across River Road.
In time the clear sky apparently took it in, forgotten
in a solution with other skies, other blue things. It's Sunday.
I just dialed—we say dialed still even though
we press numbers in on a pad—my father's number,
314-HA8-0312. It rang thirty-two times,
off the hook, as we used to say. Even back then
off the hook was an anachronism. Is that the right word?

He didn't answer. Then I had him in my mind:
He lay in the queen-size bed. The phone
was ringing on the faux French Provincial nightstand.
Mom bought it when money was good.
She used it to hold her brandy snifter of pills
when dad pumped enough Mobil gas in one year to fill
a stack of gas cans to the ionosphere.
The phone is a Christmas gift. It has big numbers.
It looks like it's for a kid to play with,
to act out his problems: *Tell me I'm good. Say something.*

Dad's down under a hundred pounds.
If he's sleeping as he used to, he's flat on his back.
His mouth must be open a little as though he's in ecstasy.
His arms lie at his side, palms up. How does he do that?
After the thirty-second ring some recorded message
between here and there said, as if a guardian angel
was breaking in, *Apparently your party
is not answering. Please hang up and call later.*

Long ago as a minor character I lay myself down
on my parents' full-size bed. My mother and my sister
were nowhere for days to be found. They were gone back
maybe to mother's mother's funeral in Nebraska.
My sister would get stung there from a bee inside
a Rose of Sharon. Or would that be me?

Those nights I tried sleeping in the same bed with my father.
You get to sleep, George, quit wiggling around, he'd say.
He'd be snoring inside five minutes. I'd stare at his mouth,
open a little like in a trance, his skin stretched smooth
over his muscled shoulders and arms.
His skin smelled a little like what I'd now call a baby's,
even the tattooed roses on his arm,
even the tattooed word, *Margaret.* I worried
he'd roll over and smash me flat as a sheet of paper.
What was in his crew-cut head then?
That nightmare of the railroad dick chasing him,
waving the two-by-four? A dream of changing oil?
Or one of his childhood pig Suzie?
Or one of Margaret hiding behind a big leaf,
her bare limbs showing?

Maybe dreams are signatures. But whose?
It's Sunday, April 2nd. I press the speed-dialer to dial
Dad, 314-HA8-0312. It's ringing now.
The *HA* stands for Harrison. It's the exchange,
the number he's had like an ID forty years.
I picture him floating on a white queen-size solution.
Is his mouth open? Last night I dreamed
he wouldn't talk and I beat him. In his face.
His mouth was slightly open. I wanted the lies
once more. That the weather was fine.
That I was good. Any minute my angel
will break in with her recorded news.
Whose messenger is she? In the dream
he did not bleed and never spoke.
It's Sunday, April 2nd. Am I in his head, carrying a stick?
Apparently my party is not answering.

Silent running

Forty years ago I drove a yellow Studebaker, a friend
on my hood. One or two more clung to the roof
and, inside, five or six of us singing, *O roll your leg over*....
Two plumes of drying barf streaked away
like painted flames from the rear side windows.
A little print of Bruegel's Peasant Wedding
hung from the clothes hook in back, to class up the act.

More than once, Sundays 2 AM we would drive like this
down the hill of Charbonnier Road until just the right speed,
and then I'd cut the flathead engine, push in the clutch,
and we'd coast powerless downhill in silence, and if in moonlight
I'd cut the headlights and we'd go in near-darkness,
all of us quieted, until a driver coming towards us got within range. Then
I'd pull the headlights on and tweak the ignition key,
the engine backfiring like a twelve-gauge
just as our fellow traveler passed by.

::

Today I am that fellow traveler jacklit
by a beast: half-young-man, half-Studebaker.
I am a flathead six-cylinder engine firing its coup de grace, headlights
giving myself the third degree.
The windows of the self rolled down, I am a blue eye
in the ditch of Charbonnier Road, I am a pink ear,
and 2 AM blows by, and a minute later 2 AM blows by,
and a minute later 2 AM blows by,
so clearly I live now and then
in Bruegel's peasant bride who herself keeps
her eyes closed, clasped hands resting in her lap, the quiet
everlasting being magnetizing the Babel of her own wedding.

::

And my friends? Jim lies spread-eagle, gripping
the chrome-winged hood ornament.
Bob and I reach out our windows, hold him by his ankles,
triangulating him. Mike and Ron lie on the roof,

grab on to the rain gutters,
friends in back reaching out to hold them by their legs.
All of us coast downhill towards the Missouri River bottomlands,
each of us holding on to another,
ignorant we would live forever, true, but in moonlight at most,
and without one word, save the wind's admonitions.

The Fitzsimmons Fund

Dear Uncle Vern: I bet you had faith in a heavenly racetrack,
not so much one with tall palms as at Santa Anita
signaling oasis or even one where horse and rider communicate
to you in trembling earth down the stretch,
not these things because they might be in
my idea of heaven, not yours.

But I bet you counted on a track where you in rolled-up shirtsleeves
could eat a rib eye *this thick* everyday at The Turf Club,
keeping an eye on your winners
down below crossing the line between uncertainty and fact,
not always winning, but never losing.
After each race three fingers of the best whiskey all around, on you.

Thank you very much for your legacy of $714.23.
I named it The Fitzsimmons Fund, after you,
and use it to rent quiet rooms to think of people, like now.
The story goes we met once—
I was six months old so the "we" is debatable.
What's your take on when someone becomes an "I"?
And was I "me" then?—
And I so impressed you that you put me
in your will? But along with sixteen others?

I think of you contemplating life (after Aunt Lucille ended
her good run of goodness—the big birthday card
from golden California addressed to "Master…,"
a never-folded dollar bill hidden inside
the nicest sentiment—and you two childless),
you done staring down the finish line,
and printed by hand (not Lucille's nun-taught graceful script)
on a sheet of Lucille's remaining personal stationery
your last will and testament as you sat up in the queen-size bed,
the estate to be equally cut up among
seventeen named beneficiaries
(Mine: "Mister…, son of…")

Before the $714.23 you were innuendo;
now you travel in a check.
Before you were a name, an address, a few conflicting stories
(Vern short for LaVern? The former wife?
The "tussle" with my dad?);
now you are a monetary action, like Social Security.
You made the book for seventeen of us beneficiaries at even odds
because you thought that was fair or because
you didn't know how to be fair
and let egalitarianism act in lieu of fairness.

Legacies like yours flesh out seventeen people and stir up wonder.
$714.23 makes us partners, but in what?
I am in a quiet room, thinking. One partner
used hers on vodka, a second partner gave hers away to Africa,
a third bought a CD getting four percent.
We are each of us worth $714.23.
How say it better?

You are not at the track eating rib eye.
In paradise a snow of torn-up tickets falls on you, standing
at the line forever, drinking beer in a plastic cup,
eating a hot dog, hardly ever winning, as it was and is here.

The Stork

Visiting friends in my birth city—actually
an acquired taste, but M.A.'s *been there.*
She let centripetal force shove her
from my car as we circled a cul-de-sac called Vale Court.
She was a wise moon. Now these two friends
illustrate how well our city's turned out.
It is as if the city is my twin. I want it to do well and not
be in rehab. It is me; so the West End is now
littered with sidewalk cafés in lieu of street people.
C'est moi. Thus I have sidewalk cafés and am free of lice.
Cafés with names such as Koko's, The Good Egg, Isis.

And many things shine and want
to dazzle me. The metallic rim of that café table, for example.
And that young woman's incisors. They both blind.
And an immaculate spittoon planted with real geraniums.
One measure of success is the degree
of disregard the successful one can imply.
Remember, the city is me. Thus the height of success
is ignorance. I ignore myself. It makes me shine
in café names, in brass containers for spit
disfigured with red blossoms.

We order strawberry crepes
and café au lait. We're done. We leave
a 50% tip. Waitress Bridgette will no doubt
remember us aloof and dazzling, until a bigger tipper.
An eternal flame demands the biggest gratuity.
Where is the statue of our city's saint? Is it
living outside memory words?
There it is, *over there* atop Art Hill
(place name, not person's) in Forest Park.
The bronze Saint Louis rides a strutting bronze horse,
its big ears pointed like those on a fixed Doberman.
Saint and horse do not shine, Saint and horse
oxidized by the century. The Saint
holds his sword high by the blade. Blade and quillions
make a cross. Is he on Crusade? *Louie, Louie.*

We are cruising my birth city. We are lost
between the Mississippi and the night.
Where shines the city's soul? Is it
in the neon *Peabody Coal* reflection
inverted on the Mississippi? Is it in streetlamps fanning out in
sulfurous rays from the Old Cathedral? Is it
from The 630' stainless Ω on the riverbank?
We're lost in my birth city.

                              What about
that neighborhood bar called The Stork wedged
like a caret into text into these old brick apartments?
We enter its apex. We are lost.
Thus ignorant we sniff the acrimony of success. Soon we may gleam.
Here in The Stork a toddler crawls on the floor. Mommy
wears a red dress, plays video poker.
Perchance she won baby here. Perchance
we shall win a family of our own.
Perchance the shy barman is my brother "washed
out of the turret with a hose."
He shall be christened Glenn. He lives
in the wedge of an apartment above the bar.
He rises there now to bring M.A. celery
and tomato juice. *Bottoms up.*
(I do this still in memory.) *Bottoms up.*
The throne of mirrored bottles around Glenn
"shone like the sun which sheds its rays far and wide."
We exit The Stork its apex. (I do this
in memory still.) We reenter the kingdom of my birth.

"Eat the rich!"

In Ohio going to visit her old parents in Illinois—
their 12' wide house trailer anchored to prairie
so the heavens have slim pickings,
thus home sweet home quivering in thunderstorms
as harps do, freezer larded full of tripe—we stop
our interstate-minded going for lunch, turkey sandwiches
on 10-grain bread preserved in wax paper.
Hungry in Milan (pronounced MY-lun), Ohio, there's zilch
for a town park but a Museum there is—closed
today, Monday—of the Birthplace of Thomas Edison, but no picnic

table. We pull into the Milan Cemetery,
spread the blue blanket on the grass which needs
a haircut, sigh, unwrapping the wax paper. How many
turkey nuggets did this turkey eat?
The 10-grain is a little stale, a super-size
Soylent Green cracker. It's paradise here, undoing
the translucent paper, refuge for the living and the dead.
I offer a few dry crumbs to Anthony Worm,
1914-, tempted to take my wax paper,
trace his tombstone's surface statement: "Called."
If he lives forever would it be *Uncalled*?

Needing to piss in Milan (pronounced MY-lun),
Ohio, there's zilch for a town toilet,
save a Johnny On The Spot just outside the cemetery
(convenient for mourners perturbed at the dead).
It's May, but not one fly inside—what do they know?
Cakes of deodorant hang. My nostrils
constrict. I lift the lid, unzip, piss into the community
waste, look straight at the translucent wall's
crayon pig's circle of a face, a balloon statement
from his snout: "I'm you." *Then, are you me?*
I ask Pig. Below him a manifesto:
"I'm ready for civil war, Eat the rich!"

In Illinois our first course is tripe soup—chewy,
especially for her old toothless father.

He is deaf, half-blind, wheel-chaired, thirty pounds less, still
young-skinned (would Pig say, *Mobil is still eating him.*
Eat them before they eat you!?) If touched just right
his shoulder would ring like the damp rim of a wine glass.
I tell him goodbye, put my hand at his back.
In my ear he whispers, *I won't forget you.*

Eating the tripe of Bill Gates shall require
endless chewing, done in remembrance of whom?
The afterlife shall be eternal cud, beautiful
code. We shall eat without end,
nourished by that which consumes us.

811 flags

The linden tree was sick, some branches
defoliated. The leaves made a tawdry lace
from innumerable mandibles. Is that
beyond *blasted*? The linden was a chewed flag
unlike the hanky-size flag fading
tacked to my big red front door. It bears a brass knocker
which once I knocked at. Please, come in.
Thanks. Nice place. Nice tree.
The hanky-size flag symbolizes our big emotion
with no period. Feelings never end.
I vowed I must save the linden or have it
cut down. May I let it be eaten? I may not.

I called Ed (the sole "arborist"
in the yellow pages). Ed arrived in a GMC pickup.
His wife stayed belted in the truck cab
reading Danielle Steele. See what I mean about feelings?
Ed walked stiff to the tree. He was
80-something. His legs of course seasoned ash.
Nice tree. It was like I'd hired dad back from the dead.
A few shekels work miracles.
Lazarus rose to consult on ascending. Then there's
Christ. Don't forget the Blessed Virgin.
Ed was thus an angel and a message. But his flight
was aberrant and his words a Turkish river.
Ed loved warblers, hated lawn chemicals, loved
photosynthesis and gypsy moths without end,
hated tree cutters and George W
without end. Ed flitted, a big warbler. Ed meandered.
Ed said, *First feed the tree.* Then I paid Ed. Ed
drove off the wrong way in his Jimmy.

So today I drill 100-plus 12 to 18-inch
deep holes in concentric circles around the linden tree.
It's like laying out a solar system. The auger
brings up rootlets clutching pebbles, clay, sand.
Nothing vertebrate. In each hole I pour in
1.5 cups of *Espoma Tree-tone (9-5-4),*

Rich in Natural Organics, A Complete Plant Food
for Shade Fruit & Ornamental Trees.

This brings us to now, our big
emotion with no period. Beyond the trees a roar.
From a child I know jet fighters. Sundays the family
would go see F-4 Phantoms take off,
feel my chest roar. This morning above the trees
three A-10 Warthogs. Tank killers.
Wing tips so close one pilot could leap from his wing
to his wingman's. That's how Ed flies.
Over me and the linden tree they roar, maybe
ten linden trees up. *Why,* and I remember—
Memorial Day. Feel my chest roar. Then only one
plane returns, waving his wings hello.

All those leaves. Today totals 811.
Which of us is not an invisible worm?
And I want to crawl into one of these small holes,
but who would tuck me in?
Who would finish drilling 12 to 18-inch deep holes
in concentric circles? Who would feed the linden?

Wh Wh Wh

I'm out on the library balcony, looking up
per usual, taking a breather from God's work,
redistributing the cornucopia's plenty,
my windowless office back there—
just a painting of an arching stone bridge done by an old friend—
tired, weary, all those dollars and cents truncated,
and my office's prints—I forgot—of Hokusai's
The Great Wave and Canaletto's *Piazza San Marco.*

Three birds—*Wh Wh Wh*—just about taking my head off,
language whose vowels are exoskeletal: carapacious; aura;
and now the smell of cooking flesh, the smell
of civilization. Of Ur, of Dresden.
Did I say that? Soon it will be lunch
once more. *Swallow your hubris,* I command myself.
Is it loaves and fishes? I shall never hunger.
Pride forever. Whole wheat, please. Thank you.
Outside a city's walls, wafts of roasted
lamb; a city is fire and burnt meat.

Out here I sit cantilevered over
students on the patio, smelling Western Civ.101.
Up here I am one of their gods. I shall rain down
pennies from on high. You're most welcome.
No windows are needed here because it's sky and its dispensations.
Is that barbecued ribs I smell?

I shall quickly meditate, becoming suffering. I'm done.

Now for something rejuvenating. I'm a stone
inside a painted arch. Shoulder to shoulder
with brother stones I hold a train aloft.
Between our legs cars speed past—*Wh wh wh.*
What is Dave grilling out there? Is that
soy pups I smell? O American Culture 202.
And now I'm strutting Piazza San Marco, not some
straniero in a big tri-corner hat,
not a vendor selling chestnuts under a torn awning,

not even a pigeon pivoting on one leg,
but that mongrel there sizing up an English Gent
on Grand Tour. A morsel, sir? Bastard!

And now I'm rowing one of Hokusai's boats.
The Great Wave bigger than Fuji in perspective.
My head's shaved like my fellow rowers'.
We're bowing with arms linked. I'm scared to death,
but my salvation is in artifice.
The Great Wave has fingers of mountain snow.

Now the patio empties for their one o'clocks.
Is that cash I smell?

To the ruins of the reputed slaughterhouse

On our walk we committed
a misdemeanor, stepping over the rusting chain.
It hung in a reddening equation, spiked between two bull pines.
First the left foot, then the right, so

(Which neighbor had said, *O, that old pile was a slaughterhouse?*
B.'s sister, who owned the black deaf dog
who curled like a welcome mat on her sidewalk?
Or G. walking little Misty until she'd beg
with both front paws, *Carry Me!?*
Did G. tell me it was a slaughterhouse from his
slouched shoulders, news from a cave?)

left foot, then the right,...,

tipping our hats to gravity, stepping past the No Trespassing sign,
(Andy later, *It felt like we had to weigh
belief, knowing a rule, breaking it.*)
then something ruptured the visual,
and squatting Andy and I saw the one who had ripped our eyes—
a foot-long suspect camouflaged in the duff of pine needles,
fleeing in an electro-chemical reaction: We would
eat him into non-snake.

(Or Mrs. S. just over the way, always well-to-do
with words, who is dogless,
Did Mrs. S. say, *O that old shambles?*)

Andy and I sidestepped the rotting
2x4s, booby-trapped with rusting nails.
Festooning the glass block windows, were those
old strings of Christmas lights?
Maybe just dead ivy, or old wire that once held a sign
advertising some special on spring lambs?
Inside the ruins the sky took over as roof, fallen on an old pickup.
It stood on four rotting tires—whitewalls!?
And a sumac—of course—sapling shooting
upward through the windshield

(and now F. the snow blower
repair guy tells me the reputed murderer
Mark Branch hid in the slaughterhouse until
he hung himself from a pine,
murderer, self-murderer, the blackening humor of a Branch
hanging until dead from a large coniferous bough.

Is that nomicide?) And next what will neighbors tell me?
That oversized woman who walks home weekdays for lunch
is the eternal mother of the murdered girl.
The ruins are assembling the neighborhood.

House afire

—for the Northampton fire victims

Fifteen fires lit up
no constellation
heaven did not fall
stars didn't shoot no

meteoric me-
teorites just one
man burning the night
touching stuff to fire

no laying on of
hands no healing no gloves
throwing crutches down
Fifteen human things

he touched & lit up—
numerous structures
and motor vehicles
a wicker basket

a wreath gloves a book
a snow globe a man-
ila folder things
we touch & don't burn

buildings we store tools
in our things with wheels
we ride in on Earth
bodies for our bodies

::

& he touched one home
a box of clothes on
neighbor Y's small porch
& Mr. Y Sr.'s

old pants did not rise
& run & Jr.'s
old shirts did not fly
bodies for bodies

::

Found: one father &
one son in the bathroom
the window ajar
ruled: "asphyxia...

smoke inhalation...
thermal injuries"
fifteen fires   two dead
one man with no rea-

son burning the night
Someone blogs "Chain him
in his apartment
then set it on fire"

A burned house burns
the next house   A house
is always burning
the next house   the next

::

Someone lays on a hand
lifts up the kneeling
Someone is a throat
Someone is a lung

Someone kisses &
blows air   Someone sees
passes on the kiss
Someone goes home   breathes

inside another
Someone rises as
air does from a leaf
To be is a breath

Best wishes, or *sortes Bushianae*

Some of us wish we were smarter and better looking
and rich and were younger.

Here few birds mornings sing. Mostly mockingbirds, starlings.
Do starlings sing? Maybe they're songbirds—goldfinches?
Mandelstam's psychic singer.

Do birds wish they were younger, rich, stronger?
To fly to the farthest of Saturn's rings?
Learn from goldfinches. Don't worry about *not*.
Think *is*. We can't be more than the world permits. We're earthlings.

What will happen to us? Who will fill the potholes?
Who will defend us against our many enemies?
Will we be rich enough to buy the stuff we need?
How high will the oceans rise? Will each of us shrivel into islands?
Will each have his own high spot?
Whose thumbs will plug the levees?

To find out some people throw grass in the air.
For example, baseball players.
Others butcher goats and read their intestines. Some buy Chevys.
Some have used chickens or espy the way crows fly.
We know friends who've paid fortune tellers.

We love surfaces. Our theory: Dig things up, *voila* becomes *voici*.
Is the inverse true? In days gone by
those lucky bastards who could read
opened a revered papyrus at random to see the future.
Nowadays the sayings
of the President of the United States shall help us ready
tomorrow. An English child asked him,
What is the White House like?
He said, *It is white.* Some people think that means
our future is Caucasian. Others say it strikes
against global warming—it's a new
ice age, totally white. Or we'll be pure,
living in paradise seeing God's face, or if

it's a Muslim world the muezzin at the mic
will sing perpetual mourning.

The new world is more than ice and white people,
more than paradise mourning.
In this future we'll run out of national debt.
Economists worry we won't have bills. Debt is value. Morning
is evening. In the red is in the black.
We'll just glance at the headlines
to get a flavor of what's moving because our assistants
read the (whole) news that very morning.
They'll brief us, then we can sound like we haven't made mistakes
even though we're confident we have, although we haven't.

We will have no deficit unless we hit the trifecta.
We will trust God speaks
through us and teach children to read so that
he or her will pass a literacy test. The first shall be first.
Oh no, we're not going to have
any casualties in any war, not even casual ones.
Ticket counters will fly out of airports
so many enemies of the Homeland
shall be slain. Speaking of slaughter, what will quench our thirst
will be the acceptable ratio of fatal shootings to non-fatal.
We will have done something about it,
all because *It is white,* this seeming tautology, this completely total,
apparent *reductio ad absurdum.* Black shall be white,
and white shall be white.

We'll give money to rich people. The last shall be last.
We shall continue to think we cannot win it.
Tomorrow they will be wrong.
Finally. Tomorrow we will find the weapons, albeit
teeth and fingernails of the past.

Nevertheless we will suffer
a great sadness. The White House track is small.
We can't run more, can't get stronger.
It shall be one of our saddest things about being President.
We won't spend a lot of time thinking

about why we do things, not any longer.
We won't be very analytical. It would set a bad precedent.
We won't think everything to death. We will master
the comedy of inductive reasoning:
Those weapons have got to be
somewhere, check every spider hole and pup tent.

Next slide please. It shows our number one
priority: We won't be resting
until we find Osama. We will all be very tired but right.
The slide show shall go on without us, running one big loop.
This foreign policy stuff will be a little frustrating. It will not be white
enough. Next slide please: Mission Accomplished.
We promise we will listen to what's been said here
even though we won't be here, right?

Wink wink. It will be one of our strengths. Ipso facto, a wish
to involve Saddam in the war on terror because
he has been willing to terrorize himself.
Saddam shall strike terror in himself. We shall aid him.

Who else shall we aid? The rich. We shall be compassionate.
We shall pass an energy bill encouraging consumption.
Some people might think that's
insane, that the future will be us thumbless peons
waiting in long lines for gas but remember debt is in the black,
our empty tank is another's full tank.

We shall stare the future in his face and say, *Bring them on,*
all those tomorrow's camouflaged
as roadside bombs, but don't you worry now—
we'll be out of gas. The waters shall rise, our enemies shall drown.
They can't even dog paddle. Their IUD's will fizzle.

Our mornings shall rise brightly, a big Caucasian face
smiling providentially upon us
making our new papyrus high and dry on little islands.
We dare not disturb the surface, for therein lies water
and no one will have reinvented
the sump pump, much less electricity.

Tripe shall be our national dish, inasmuch as
farm animals will have been bred
with gigantic intestines, the better to tell our futures,
the poorer to gauge our past. A past of broken levees—
since stoppered with the superfluous digits of immigrants—
and potholes—dittoed. We shall prize starlings at last
for three things: their ideal of congregating behavior,
their skill at eating tripe, their morning song which we shall believe
sounds like: *there is here, there is here.*

Happy genius of my household

Bile in the throat. Couldn't sleep. My body
not DNA'd for coffee or wine. Let's say it's 3 am
in that crevice—or is it crevasse?—of netherworldliness
betwixt and between THIS and THAT.
Did the ghost balloon up from *mea corpus delicti* on the bed?
Who was that masked man?
All for 4 ounces tap water, ½ teaspoon bicarbonate of soda.
Stir briskly. Netherworldly libation.

Full moonlight on the snow made us
the moon's moon, filled the night kitchen
with goddedness. Glass of bicarbonate half-emptyful.
Night kitchen's own life. Not mine. Not ours.
My eyeglasses back in the day, I down the beaker of bicarbonate
and out the kitchen window   *If when my wife is sleeping*
dark creature four-legged long-tailed
runs from the whitened garden plot   *and the baby and Kathleen*
where mint grew without self control
kitty corner to the Lesser Beyond   *are sleeping*
behind the moonlit shed.
No one to follow my eyes, say *Yes, I saw it,*
no one to hand me my ghost, say *Come back to bed,*
come back to yourself, to your senses. Come back to us.

My coffee mug stood on its own, 3 AM moonlight.
The kitchen does not kneel. Does not lick.
The kitchen window is at me. Sore throat says,
What was that dark creature?
Was it feline? Was it canine? *It's like this. It's that.*
The four-legged, long-tailed creature wrote a / in the moonlit snow.
The reader never sleeps.

Beyond the Missouri sky

—after Charlie Haden and Pat Metheny

A man over a keyboard waits for what
the interstices dish up. He'll chew that, eating waiting.
A torch song of knotted string would be nice,
a chord out of a cord.
Or thunderbolt from cumulus, zig of light
zagging down from his head to fingers.

A man holds his fingers, being chewed.
Sounds go unreferenced outside his windows, tires holding notes
up in upper registers, wind explicating a white oak.
It cowers over the neighbor's where a man hides,
spends life—*yours, mine*—in his cellar. Before dawn promises,
his cellar window sends an incandescent slit—

I walk the tightrope
of light to the cellarman's window,
being neighborly. He's nowhere seen. Implication,
make the man. There's his oxygen tank. There's his stale smoke
emanating from cellar walls, his short ceiling
taking the measure of the man. Patty-cake him into life.

Where the wall ends, light takes over. Here he walks,
growing larger, like love. He ducks his head under a beam,
puts on his oxygen mask. Fear is scrawled
in his face like the letter 'B.'
Wrinkles cinch his lips, wrinkles
cinch his eyes. Thirty-six years in his cellar. Walk back up
the tightrope of light, make no music, no word.

At the Marconi Station

O, God, another beautiful ocean view.
What's this, the 57th time this week?
My gauge goes numb. Beauty, friends, is boring.
It's big and blue with little facets of semi-preciousness.
The horizon is cursive. That dark spot is a big ship.
No doubt sailors are gesturing to us.

On this bluff Marconi got his message: ...
That's what England had to say.
The station's a mess on the beach like a — — — what?
Bare ruined choir? Rotting Victorian paragraph?
The Atlantic is big and patient, digesting eight more inches a year.
That's a good appetite. Only a millennium
and the ruins will be Atlanticized. — — — mama.

But what's that? Three beds of kelp? Swimming kelp?
Each with a head that's coming out of water?
The Atlantic has three faces, not just one
face of the waters, not just "little facets."
Are you gods? Three-personned god?
Faith, hope, and charity? Triton and friends?

The larger one holds his head steady
on the surface despite the breaking waves and stares.
His eyes articulate in eyesockets. *I am no threat to you,
Mister Seal.* His eyes are eightballs.
Do you weep often? There're those dark channels
from your eyes. Bark once for yes,
bark twice for no. OK, don't bark. The other two
are smaller and stay behind him.

What do you know of humans? We probably stink.
Saltwater is a human solution.
Once I drove to the dock of the bay. I pissed in the ocean,
watching the tide roll away.
You can hear us, right? You can hear turbines turning
giant propellers? Chinese water torture?

Now they slowly submerge and look kelp-like again.
Now I can't see them. Don't leave me.
I want to hold the smallest one in my arms.
Now I may break.
We have no common language. If so, I would sit down
at The People's Pint with Mister Seal,
I would "wet/Right many a nipperkin."
We meet in signs in dirt in water
at the edge of this inundated garden.
Morse's decoded first message demands,
What hath God wrought?...

Piseco Lake, the Empire State

I'm lying on a twin bed, staring back
at the beech tree outside the second-story window.
The tree has been plated in some semi-precious metal.
Soon enough it will be coal
in the night, or a fossil for the time being,
like those ferns found inside stones
but for now the western sun lights it up. For now
it stares me down. I close my eyes
a second and it's there in negative, framed
in my eyes by the shadow window.

I want to exercise patience. To lie here.
My head pillowed as if on a tuft of moss
as long as it takes for the tree to go invisible, for it to be
coaled. For all of us to be.

And the house is quieted, the others off also
taking pleasure from here and now,
honoring it, letting it make us
good. There is Dave's graveled footstep
and the chatting paws of the puppy
Dr. Jazz, their six legs walking to the old boathouse.
Dave will throw a stick from the concrete dock into
the water. Dr. Jazz will whine
at his incapacity to swim. He'll run along
the tiny beach to find a substitute stick.
He'll bring it to Dave who will throw it also into the lake.
Mean Dave, Dr. Jazz will whine.

And Lee must be kayaking one last time down
the lakeshore, half of her below waterline.
I think she pauses in twilight and lets the lake's
wavelets jostle her, I think
she lets herself drift. She wants to feel
useless. Her hands in water solicit whatever.

And from the patio Anita watches the loon
suddenly submerge leaving a coil of wavelets.
Its call had beckoned her thrice. Will she follow it?

How can she? It comes from every direction,
and now she sees it bob back
to the surface, a hundred—two hundred—feet distant.
She will tell me of the loon later as we lie
waiting in our twin beds for sleep. But here and now

the beech tree is almost invisible,
almost one coal with the night, almost pure
retina tree. Its remembered bronzed branches
a history of pleasure and pain:
the bronze scepter, the wooden cudgel.
How pleasure incorporates tree lake mountain
into us. How the sensation of
dog friend loon spreads across us, fleshes us out.

Now voices mumble below this twin bed
as if from below a lake's surface, the house unquieted
and just like that the beech tree is lit
as if from footlights, as if from a fire at the trunk's base.
Someone must have turned the kitchen light on
for a bed-time snack, a sip of wine.
All three voices Dave Lee Anita (not to mention
the puppy Dr. Jazz) bubbling up to me,
I await. The kitchen light doused. The beech tree
coaled. A whisper of her feet on the carpet.
Her loon's underwater adventures. The tree
to go invisible. And then to climb it.

Hotel Oceania

— for Anita

This afternoon more snow. It takes forever
to touch its kin. I thought for a moment
I would help it fall. Pull it down. But the sky is in back of it.

I don't know much about your soul, even after ten thousand nights.
In this photo I brought with me you look like someone else.
Almost like you when I'm not around.
And I'm the one who released the shutter
and fixed eternity with your face and legs.
You sit at the foot of the bed,
your arms in back propping you up. You've hitched
your skirt up to show your legs.
Where does a soul reside? In a hotel room? In legs? In eyes I know
the color of spring mint but in the photo
narrowed to slits? In teeth bared in a smile?

Everything on the planet chipped in to make you joyous this instant.
The new millennium that fed us and did not
bomb us is in your upturned lips.
That Roman alley's *motos* and barred shrine
to the Madonna, it's in your smile.
The open elevator with room for just
us two. Stephano's lesson on the "r."
The "3" hanging loosely on our door. Our room's
bedbugs. The blood on our sheet.
All in your joyous eyes narrowed to slits. All
in your smile. All in your legs.

But you gave more than the world gave. You said,
I am more than I am
and in giving gave the world's gifts. You smile. Your eyes narrow.
Your lips turn up at baring your legs, joy
of exhibiting more than you are.
And this instant's revelation lets eternity
bare its legs. Anytime, anywhere,
tomorrow is possible. You open
your mint-green eyes. You walk in them.

Acknowledgments

"The Cloud of Unknowing," "Belladonna," "The Grand Burlesque," "Taking Leave of St. Louis," "One Hundred and Fifty Springs in Hannibal," "Some Reasons for Everything," "On the Lookout for Neighbors," "Everybody's Business," "Little Cloud of Dust," "Red Cottage," "The Isle of Lepers," "Over *Voice of America*, "Singing Tree," "In the Stars," "Swimming at Night," "Altar Boys," "The Great Bear over Grand Junction, Colorado," and "Pass It On" are from Dennis Finnell's *Red Cottage,* copyright 1991. Reprinted by permission of the University of Massachusetts Press.

"Headless Horseman," "On The Taconic Parkway At Nine Partners' Road," "Grotto," "Cupola," "Kiss," "The Generic Manifesto," "Rapunzel, Rapunzel," "Invasions of Privacies," "Hannibal, Revisited," "Ballade, U.S.A.," "Acmeist," "Our Epictetus," "Rapunzel, Again," "The Irish Wilderness," "Tongue. The End of the World Is Roadless. Exile." and "Real Poetik" are from Dennis Finnell's *Belovèd Beast,* copyright 1995. Reprinted by permission of the University of Georgia Press.

"Some of you look into this, my mouth," "Start our eyes," "Scratch, sniff," "Come, endure," "Out of mouths," "Her kiss evaporates, his testimony calcifies," "Ultimata," "Conspirators, speaking," "Aorta, keeping the white-caps white," are from Dennis Finnell's *The Gauguin Answer Sheet,* copyright 2001. Reprinted by permission of the University of Georgia Press.

"Noise enters," "Who's there but yesteryear," "Tell why once a girl," "The season began inauspiciously," "To return," "It's staring at it," "Overdid the wise-acre," "Beauty dwarf pretty face," "Accord," "A tube with lenses," "Here in you the shattered surrounds us," "Whose future is white?" "If a nation," "The unterraced," "Love dark," "Heaven stop here for sex," "This little creature," "It's time," and "To sit down on a tree stump," "Light," "Mouth of truths," "Father of the man," "Silent running," "The Fitzsimmons Fund," "The Stork," "'Eat the rich!'" "811 flags," "Wh Wh Wh," "To the ruins of the reputed slaughterhouse," "House afire," "Best wishes, or *sortes Bushianae,*" "Happy genius of my household," "Beyond the Missouri sky," "At the Marconi Station," "Piseco Lake, the Empire State," and "Hotel Oceania" are from Dennis Finnell's *Ruins Assembling,* copyright 2014. Reprinted by permission of Shape&Nature Press.

I am grateful to the editors of the following publications in which some of these poems, in whole or in part, originally appeared, sometimes in different forms or with different titles:

RED COTTAGE

The Agni Review: "Everybody's Business"
The Chariton Review: "Altar Boys," "One Hundred and Fifty Springs in
    Hannibal," "Taking Leave of St. Louis"
College English: "Red Cottage"
Denver Quarterly: "Over *Voice of America*"
Intro 11: "Some Reasons for Everything"
New England Review and Bread Loaf Quarterly: "The Great Bear over Grand
    Junction, Colorado"
The New Republic: "The Cloud of Unknowing"
Poetry East: "Singing Tree"
River City: "Pass It On"
Tar River Poetry: "Belladonna"

BELOVÈD BEAST

American Literary Review: "Grotto," "On the Taconic Parkway at Nine
    Partners' Road"
Denver Quarterly: "The Irish Wilderness," "Real Poetik"
The Illinois Review: "The Generic Manifesto," "Rapunzel, Rapunzel"
Laurel Review: "Ballade, U.S.A.," "Invasions of Privacies"
The Massachusetts Review: "Acmeist"
New Letters: "Hannibal, Revisited"
Pequod: "Kiss"
Santa Clara Review: "Our Epictetus," "Rapunzel, Again"

THE GAUGUIN ANSWER SHEET

The Blue Moon Review: A Triannual Online Review of the Literary Arts: "Come,
    endure" and "Aorta, keeping the whitecaps white," both in slightly
    different form.
Colorado Review: "Some of you look into this, my mouth" and "Start our
    eyes" appeared in different form and under different titles.
Interim: "Conspirators, speaking"

RUINS ASSEMBLING

Colorado Review: "Wh wh wh," "Hotel Oceania," "Piseco Lake, the Empire
    State," "The Fitzsimmons Fund"
Denver Quarterly: "Father of the man"

Fence: "To the ruins of the reputed slaughterhouse"
Harpur Palate: "Best wishes, or *sortes Bushinae*"
Interim: "811 flags," "At the Marconi Station," "The Stork"
The Massachusetts Review: "House afire"
New Letters: "Silent running"
POOL: "Light"

About FutureCycle Press

FutureCycle Press is dedicated to publishing lasting English-language poetry books, chapbooks, and anthologies in both print-on-demand and digital (ebook) formats. Founded in 2007 by long-time independent editor/publishers and partners Diane Kistner and Robert S. King, the press incorporated as a nonprofit in 2012. A number of our editors are distinguished poets and writers in their own right, and we have been actively involved in the small press movement going back to the early seventies.

The FutureCycle Poetry Book Prize and honorarium is awarded annually for the best full-length volume of poetry we publish in a calendar year. Introduced in 2013, our Good Works projects are anthologies devoted to issues of universal significance, with all proceeds donated to a related worthy cause. Our Selected Poems series highlights contemporary poets with a substantial body of work to their credit; with this series we strive to resurrect work that has had limited distribution and is now out of print.

We are dedicated to giving all of the authors we publish the care their work deserves, making our catalog of titles the most diverse and distinguished it can be, and paying forward any earnings to fund more great books.

We've learned a few things about independent publishing over the years. We've also evolved a unique, resilient publishing model that allows us to focus mainly on vetting and preserving for posterity the most books of exceptional quality without becoming overwhelmed with bookkeeping and mailing, fundraising activities, or taxing editorial and production "bubbles." To find out more about what we are doing, come see us at www.futurecycle.org.

The FutureCycle Poetry Book Prize

All full-length original volumes of poetry published by FutureCycle Press in a given calendar year are considered for the annual FutureCycle Poetry Book Prize. This allows us to consider each submission on its own merits, outside of the context of a contest. Too, the judges see the finished book, which will have benefitted from the beautiful book design and strong editorial gloss we are famous for.

The book ranked the best in judging is announced as the prize-winner in the subsequent year. There is no fixed monetary award; instead, the winning poet receives an honorarium of 20% of the total net royalties from all poetry books and chapbooks the press sold online in the year the winning book was published. The winner is also accorded the honor of being on the panel of judges for the next year's competition; all judges receive copies of all contending books to keep for their personal library.

www.ingramcontent.com/pod-product-compliance
Lightning Source LLC
Chambersburg PA
CBHW072142090426
42739CB00013B/3253